THE SINAI MYTH

Books by Andrew M. Greeley:

AND YOUNG MEN SHALL SEE VISIONS
THE CATHOLIC EXPERIENCE
THE CHANGING CATHOLIC COLLEGE
THE CHURCH AND THE SUBURBS
COME BLOW YOUR MIND WITH ME
THE CRUCIBLE OF CHANGE
THE EDUCATION OF CATHOLIC AMERICANS (with Peter H. Rossi)
THE FRIENDSHIP GAME
A FUTURE TO HOPE IN
THE HESITANT PILGRIM: American Catholicism after the Council
THE JESUS MYTH
LETTERS TO NANCY
LIFE FOR A WANDERER
NEW HORIZONS FOR THE PRIESTHOOD
PRIESTS IN THE UNITED STATES: Reflections on a Survey
RELIGION AND CAREER
RELIGION IN THE YEAR 2000
THE SINAI MYTH
THAT MOST DISTRESSFUL NATION: The Taming of the American
   Irish
UNCERTAIN TRUMPET
WHAT A MODERN CATHOLIC BELIEVES ABOUT GOD
WHY CAN'T THEY BE LIKE US? Ethnic Conflict in America

ANDREW M. GREELEY
The Sinai Myth

1972

Doubleday & Company, Inc., Garden City, New York

ISBN: 0-385-01468-6
Library of Congress Catalog Card Number 72-79390
Copyright © 1972 by Andrew M. Greeley
All Rights Reserved
Printed in the United States of America

CONTENTS

THE GOD OF THE FRUITFUL
MOUNTAIN:
THE SINAI MYTH

INTRODUCTION

From the mists of prehistory between the thirteenth and eighth centuries B.C. there emerged in Palestine a people with a strikingly different religious tradition. A nomadic and illiterate people, they did not write their experience of God on paper for hundreds of years. When the oral tradition finally did become literary, it was composed of complex tribal laws; ancient poems, chants, and oracles; fables, parables, and legends from a distant past.

This collection of different source materials creates a great problem for our own very literal-minded age. Our understanding of the sources must begin with the realization that the documents which we have are an attempt to record an oral tradition, which in its turn was an attempt to record an extraordinary religious experience. No description of a religious experience is adequate even if it is an individual experience at one particular time and place. The Israelite traditions were an endeavor to record the religious experience of a whole people over a considerable period of time. We may not find their experiences particularly attractive or helpful or we may find them deeply moving. In either case we cannot begin to do justice to the Israelites or their traditions until we realize that we are dealing with something more than a bizarre collection of texts, some of which are confusing, some obscure, and some downright unedifying. In the documents we are confronting an experience of God, and before we do justice to the Israelites we must strive to understand as best we can the nature of that experience. Who was the God that the Israelites encountered in their going out of Egypt? At the foot of Sinai? Upon entering the Promised Land? What did this central religious symbol of the Jewish religion have to say about the nature and purpose of human life?

It is only when we attempt to answer these questions that we encounter the Israelite heritage. Agonizing over where the "Red" or the "Reed" Sea was or what the nature of the disaster that befell the army of the Pharaoh was or where Mount Sinai was or what sort of natural explanation there can be for the manna in the desert is quite beside the point. One can find natural explanations for the manna and the parting of the waters or one can dismiss them as fables. One can assume that the voice of Yahweh really was heard from the top of Sinai (wherever it might have been) or one can say that the Israelites witnessed a volcanic eruption. Finally, one can conclude that the whole Sinai story is a legend made up by clever priests in the eighth century B.C. (None of these explanations seem to be satisfactory to me, incidentally.) But having made these judgments about the description of the Sinai event, we have only begun our work. The critical question is not how did Sinai occur but what does it mean? We cannot understand the Israelites and their tradition unless we first of all understand the meaning of Sinai.

Going out of Egypt, encountering Yahweh in the desert, and entering Palestine were the experiences which gave the Israelites their God and made them a people. Those three experiences constitute the core of the Israelite tradition, and whatever may be said about the historical nature of those events as they come down to us in the Israelite documents, it must be admitted that the nineteenth and twentieth chapters of the book of Exodus record the center of that tradition.

The experience of God on Sinai became the decisive symbol in Israelite religion and theology. If we wish to understand Israel we must understand Sinai. Judaism as we know it today began with the experience recorded in those two chapters of Exodus, and Christianity can claim to be nothing else but a continuation of the Sinai experience. If someone from the outside wishes to understand either Judaism or Christianity he must first comprehend Sinai; and if the Jew or the Christian wishes to understand who and what he is, he, too, must comprehend Sinai. For on that mountain, El Shaddai, the God of the Fruitful Mountain, became Yahweh, the One Who Causes Things to Be; and the history of the human race was changed decisively.[1]

This book, then, is an attempt to understand the Sinai event as recorded in the nineteenth and twentieth chapters of the book of Exodus.

Let me conclude this introduction with a word about the kind of book this is. It is certainly not an exercise in academic theology because I am not a theologian. Nor is it the work of a professional exegete, because while I have immense respect for their skills, I do not possess them. I have consulted the exegetes, both their books and their persons. It is possible that I have misunderstood them in some respects, but I do not think it likely

[1] There are various translations given for "El Shaddai": the God of the Mountain, the God of the Fruitful Mountain, or even the God of the Breast. I might have chosen the third translation as the title for this book. It emphasizes the fertility cult aspect of pre-Sinai religion and would not be inappropriate given the passionate nature of the relationship between Yahweh and his people. I think, however, that it might not be acceptable in contemporary religious book publishing. I shall explore this aspect of Yahweh in a later chapter.

that I have misunderstood the basic religious symbolism of chapters 19 and 20 of the book of Exodus. My reflections on those symbols are my own. They are submitted to the reader not as an apodictic interpretation of the symbols but for whatever use they may be to the reader's own reflections.

If anything, the book is an exercise in sociology, although scarcely of the sort one would submit to *The American Sociological Review*. It is a search for meaning, an attempt to determine what a given set of religious symbols means, what basis these symbols provide for "a pact against chaos and death," as Peter Berger has put it. Paradoxically enough, the sociologist approaches religion with the same question that the deeply religious man asks: What do these sets of religious symbols really mean? I will scarcely claim that this book is an exercise in scholarly sociology, but I will assert that if I were not a sociologist and had not had the experience of more than a decade of sociological research, I do not think I would have come to ask the question that I am trying to ask in this volume.

Is the book an exercise in "popularization"? I am not sure what that word really means, though it has a certain pejorative sense (particularly when used by book reviewers) that I would not accept. If "popularization" means only the absence of basic research, then I suppose that it is clear that this book is "popularized." "Popularization" may also imply that a work is unserious and watered down, something light and frothy that an author serves up to people who are not as intelligent as he and surely not as intelligent as his academic colleagues. If this is what is meant by "popularization"—and I think such a connotation is usually intended—then this book is not "popular."

This volume is a deadly serious attempt to cope with some of the most fundamental religious questions human beings can ask. Whether the book is profound is not for me to say; I do not equate seriousness or profundity with either obscurity or the scholarly apparatus. I refuse to accept the right of academics and their fellow travelers to define what is important and serious and at the same time to insist that the only worthwhile things are written principally for scholars.

It is important to make this point, I think, at the beginning of any attempt at religious interpretation. We cannot approach serious religious interpretation without the assistance of archaeologists, historians, linguists, exegetes, theologians. But if we cannot understand religious symbols without the assistance of such scholars, we should not equate their brilliant and skillful scholarly work with religion or faith and our efforts to implement religious symbols in our lives. Yahweh did not write a Ph.D. dissertation on Sinai, and Moses never produced an article for a learned journal. Religion, today at least, presupposes solid scholarship, but it does not and cannot stop there.

CHAPTER 1

SINAI AS TURNING POINT

One of my friends was horrified when he heard I was doing a book "about the Ten Commandments." "No one," he protested, "is interested in them any more."

What can one say in response to such a comment? It is certainly true that our catechisms and our moral theology books turned the Ten Commandments into a rigid ethical code from which we were supposed to deduce detailed norms for all our decisions about behavior. Such inflexible codes of behavior became first oppressive and then irrelevant. If it be true that no one is interested in the Ten Commandments, the reason may well be that the Decalogue was converted into a harsh, legalistic code despite Yahweh and Jesus. The problem still remains: Why did something, now judged to be so inhuman, have such tremendous importance to so many people for so long?

The Sinai experience was not fundamentally an ethical vision at all. It was a religious event, an encounter of man with God. The ethical code which emerged from that encounter was simple, not especially original, and rather of secondary importance. In our catechism classes and in our moral theology courses we skipped over the first three or four commandments rapidly. Graven images were no problem, taking God's name in vain was only a venial sin, not very many people used Ouija boards or went to fortunetellers, and servile work on Sunday was so difficult to define that nobody paid much attention to it. The really important commandments, the ones on which we spent most of our time, were the seventh, eighth, and ninth. Theft, injustice, and adultery—those were the things worth worrying about!

But in fact the context of the Sinai covenant shows that it is the first three commandments that really count. If one wishes to understand the religious experience of Sinai, one must understand them.

If I am told that no one is interested in the Decalogue as a symbol of a profound religious experience whose impact is still very much with us, I am astonished. There are, of course, people who believe that there is nothing to be learned from the past. They can take Margaret Mead seriously when she asserts that the "now" generation has its roots in the future, not the past; and they can take Alvin Toffler seriously when he argues that "future shock" has eliminated almost all stability and continuity from human society. It would seem to me, however, that anyone with a moderate amount of education or intelligence must be aware that we are all creatures of our past heritages. Indeed, even the rejection of our heritage is normally done in the categories the heritage provides for us. If one turns away, for example, from the Jewish or the Christian religious traditions, one generally does so in terms of a messianic vision of the future of the human race—quite unaware that if it were not for the Jewish and Christian heritages, the human race would be totally lacking messianic concepts. Western man thinks about the future only because somewhere in his past there was a covenant that was a promise. We have the vocabulary and the thought patterns to discuss "future shock" only because more than three millennia ago some of our spiritual ancestors encountered a God who, unlike the other gods around him, seemed more concerned with the future than he was with the past.

But this book is not written to argue with those who say that the past is unimportant. It is for those who wish to respond to the present religious situation in which they find themselves and who wonder whether the symbols available to them from their heritage can have meaning for them now. The Sinai experience and the Decalogue which records it are unquestionably critical religious symbols that are part of our heritage. Before we reject them we should at least know what they mean.

The accounts that we have available to us in the book of Exodus are obviously highly stylized traditions passed on first by word of mouth and then a number of different written traditions. They are filled with both theological reflection and religious exhortation. It is extremely difficult to get beyond these documents to an understanding of the actual historical events. However, modern scholars are inclined to agree that the stylized accounts of the book of Exodus are not mere fables; that they describe people who actually existed and events which really occurred, although they describe them in a very different way from what we would expect historical narrative to be today.

It would appear that following the defeat of the Hyksos invaders (about 1560), the Egyptian Pharaohs began to reestablish their empire. In the process they did battle with some of the "foreigners," the Apiru, who had settled in Egypt and just outside its borders. Some of these Apiru or Hebrews did apparently leave Egypt during the thirteenth century B.C., probably escaping from an Egyptian military detachment that was thrown into disarray by a natural disturbance in the marshlands between Egypt and the Sinai peninsula. At some later point in history, this tribe (or perhaps a collection of tribal elements) combined with other tribes that lived in the desert beyond the borders of Palestine and invaded that land. Some of those who left Egypt, or perhaps some of the other tribal components whom they later encountered, had a traumatic religious experience near a sacred mountain, which may have been in any of a number of places in the Sinai peninsula. (If you require a volcanic mountain, then it has to be on the eastern side of Sinai near the Gulf of Aqabah; if you trust early Christian or even late pre-Christian tradition, then it was the mountain called the Mountain of Moses in the southwestern part of Sinai. Even the Old Testament sources seem uncertain as to where the mountain really was.)

It is entirely possible that the going out of Egypt was experienced by one tribe and Sinai was experienced by another, while the occupation of Palestine was experienced by considerable numbers of people who were part of neither the Exodus nor the Sinai encounter. These questions are fascinating historical and archaeological issues, but they are rather less important in terms of religious symbolism. By the time we meet the twelve tribes of Israel, they are a religious confederation, an amphictyony. Whatever the historical events were that gave rise to the sense of a common religious experience, this sense was well established in the twelve tribes by the time we are able to deal with them on the basis of historical records. It was also that sense which fundamentally constituted them as people.

It is a mistake, then, to think of the Israelite religious experience as one that occurred only in a given place and to a specific number of people. It happened over time, several centuries perhaps, and in varying ways to a whole population. Exodus and Sinai were decisive components of this religious experience in both constituting it and symbolizing it, but they do not represent the totality of the experience as it historically occurred.

How many people were at the foot of Sinai? Were

they the same people who went out of Egypt? Was Moses really there? Was there a volcanic eruption or was there a thunderstorm? Did the people imagine that they heard the voice of Yahweh? Or were the sounds of natural phenomena "interpreted" for them by their leaders? Obviously, certain answers to these questions are not possible now. In all likelihood they will never be possible, and while these questions are legitimate historically, they are not especially important from the religious viewpoint. More important than how Israel came to believe that Yahweh was its God is the question of what kind of God he is. The children of Israel experienced over a period of time a number of dramatic events which forced them to interpret the nature of their relationship to the Really Real. The Sinai symbol and the covenant theology which flows from it were the way Israel tied together its striking experiences, interpreted them, and used them as a basis for creating a religious and national unity. Rather than to inquire what really happened at Sinai, the important question to ask is what does Sinai really mean?

However obscure the historical events may be, there can be no doubt that the religious experience which occurred at Sinai and which is embodied in the traditional interpretation of the events is absolutely unique. Let us quickly admit that the Israelite religion did not spring into being completely free from the influence of the culture of which it was a part. Its poetry and its creation myths owe something in language if not in content to the Semite and Babylonian myths which pervaded the ancient Near East. The etymological roots of the name "Yahweh" are obscure but must be located in the cultural heritage of the Israelites or in those cultures that influenced them. It is possible that Israelite monotheism was influenced by the Egyptian monotheism of the heretic Pharaoh Ikhnaton (Amenophis IV), who lived probably a century before Moses. It is also highly probable that in its beginnings the religion of Yahweh did not deny the existence of other gods. The Yahweh who was encountered in the desert was not the only god or even necessarily the chief of the gods. What he was—and this is the decisive part—was a god totally different from any other.

Furthermore, let us be prepared to admit that Yahweh owed something to the mountain gods of the wandering Semitic tribesmen and to the personal gods of family and clan. Indeed, it is quite obvious that the collectors of the Old Testament documents equate Yahweh with the personal and family gods of the patriarchs who went before them.

But having made all these admissions of limitation, it still must be asserted that the encounter of Israel with Yahweh was an absolutely unique religious experience. It was unlike anything else in the ancient world. It took a long time for Israel to understand the meaning of its encounter with Yahweh. (And those of us who are still Israelites, real or spiritual, have yet to exhaust the full meaning of that encounter.) But the uniqueness of Israel's experience is as clear in the first written records of it as in the later sophistication, interpretation, and elaboration of it.

This book assumes that most of the old battles are over, that we no longer have to argue about whether Genesis (which is a book of secondary importance compared to Exodus) is scientific history, about whether Moses really lived, and about whether the book of Numbers was really jotted down in the shadow of Sinai. I take it that having put aside such relatively trivial questions, we can address ourselves to the fundamental question that the Sinai symbol raises for us: What is the nature of the relationship it describes between man and God?

Religious symbols must be explored and interpreted to see what they tell us about God, about the fundamental nature of the universe, and about the purpose of human

life. Every religious symbol attempts to offer an interpretation of the human condition, and the fundamental
question we must ask about a religious symbol is not
whether it teaches us truth but whether it provides useful insights into the nature of the Real. All human religious symbols are valid in the sense that they all shed
some light on the human condition. The theologian
Schubert Ogden offers us the following principle of the
verifiability of religious symbols: "Mythical assertions are
true insofar as they so explicate our unforfeitable assurance that life is worth while that the undertanding of
faith they represent cannot be falsified by the essential
conditions of life itself."[1] Ogden goes on to say:

> The reality with which mythical assertions must come
> to terms is not the everchanging world disclosed by
> our senses, but our own existence as selves, as those
> who, whatever their external perceptions, always ex-
> perience themselves and the world as finite-free parts
> of an infinite whole. It is for this reason that mythical
> assertions, when true, express an understanding of
> faith which not only *is* not falsified by our experi-
> ence, but also *can* not be so falsified.[2]

Following Ogden's norm, what we must ask of the Sinai
experience is to what extent it confirms our own basic
conviction about the worth and purpose and dignity of
humankind. If the Sinai myth does indeed powerfully
"re-present" (to use Ogden's word) this primordial religious conviction for us, then it has validity not only for
people who first experience it but for those of us who
approach it today once again. What we must do is to
ask first of all, what does Sinai really mean? And, second,
what does Sinai mean for *us?* To anticipate somewhat the

[1] Schubert Ogden, *The Reality of God and Other Essays*. New
York: Harper & Row, 1966, p. 116.
[2] Ibid., p. 117.

conclusion of this book, it means infinitely more than a series of negative prohibitions. It is, rather, a revelation of God's love for man.

I am not suggesting that we come to the foot of Sinai to ask Yahweh for specific answers on issues like birth control, war, racial justice, and pollution. If the pertinence and utility of a religious symbol depends on the capacity of that symbol to provide simple, clear, and direct answers for specific social and ethical problems, then forget about the God of the Fruitful Mountain, because he doesn't have them—but then neither does any other god, or at least no other god who respects the intelligence and freedom of his followers.

Nor should we ask if Yahweh is a revolutionary. In some sense he is; certainly human religion has never quite been the same since the Sinai encounter. But if it is required for Yahweh to be "relevant," that he lay down a concrete program for overthrowing the Establishment (whatever that may be), then Yahweh is no revolutionary. He did not like idolatry and he still doesn't. Any attempt to reduce him to a specific program or a specific set of answers is idolatry, precisely because it absolutizes the relative; it turns that which is contingent and problematic into something that is eternal and unquestionable. Of this sort of thing Yahweh will have no part.

If we are to make a pilgrimage to the foot of Sinai at all, our purpose must be to find out what Yahweh says about the meaning and purpose of human existence; then we must determine what the insights we obtain from listening to Yahweh mean for our own lives.

If we wish to approach with reverence, respect, and intelligence the religious symbols which are part of our heritage, we must avoid two extremes. First of all, we must not become so bogged down in the cultural particularities of the situation in which the symbol was first used that we lose sight of its possible pertinence for our own lives. On the other hand, we must not twist that symbol so out of its own proper context as to force it to provide detailed and literal instructions for our own behavior. The first approach is that of the history of religions, which brilliantly and with fantastic displays of erudition describes the religious symbol in its proper context and asks no questions about what challenge the symbol may pose for the life of the analyst. The second approach is that of fundamentalism, which thinks, for example, that Yahweh's dealing with the Amorites is appropriate guidance for our dealing with Communists. In the historical approach, the symbol is left safely in its context; fundamentalism pulls it completely out of context.

Interpretation asks what the symbol tells us about man, God, reality, purpose, meaning, and community. The interpretive art is a difficult one, though I think not necessarily more difficult today than it has ever been. Any of those of us who engage in interpretation—and I suppose all religious people do—should be aware of the tentative and transitory nature of our interpretations. The best we can do is to say that the religious symbol as we understand it seems to mean certain things for us now. Beyond that we must be very wary of imposing our interpretations either on future generations or demanding them of prior ones.[3]

This book is an exercise in interpretation from the perspective of a schismatic Yahwistic sect founded by one Jesus of Nazareth, who claimed to have a unique relation-

[3] I should like to make it clear that I do not think our own interpretations can ignore those of the past. If every generation must return to the primal religious symbols, it can do so with intelligence, I think, only if it has respect and reverence for how previous generations have dealt with the symbols. It is the most stupid sort of temporal ethnocentrism to refuse to learn from the wisdom of the past. It is also the most stupid sort of religious timidity to refuse to attempt to go beyond the interpretations of the past in our search for meaning.

ship with Yahweh. The Israelite experience with Yahweh
was an ongoing one. In their encounters with him in
Exodus and on Sinai they discovered that Yahweh was a
God of history, a God who acts. So, necessarily, he was
to be encountered again and again. It was the claim of
the Christians to have had a new experience of Yahweh
as he manifested himself in Jesus. Surely, it was not an
experience that negated the Sinai encounter but one that
continued to develop and enrich it. Christianity—whether
some Christians like it or not—is a Yahwistic religion. It
may very well represent a notable leap beyond the Sinai
symbol, but it was a leap that could only occur in the
religious tradition of which Sinai was the central event.
From one point of view, the quantum leap of human
understanding in which El Shaddai became Yahweh was
an even greater one than that represented by the Easter
experience of the early Christians. To put the issue in a
schematic and oversimplified form: On Sinai we learned
that God loves us; in the cross and resurrection we
learned how much he loves us.

I have repeatedly used the words "experience" and "encounter." Let me make it clear that I am not speaking
about religious "feeling" or religious sentiment. I am talking about a profound human insight that pervades the
whole person, intellect, and feeling. The "experience" I
have in mind is a revelatory one, or, perhaps more precisely, a response to a revelation that one perceives as
having occurred. It is not merely the subjective experience
of the modernist but rather a response to objective reality.

But the question may be pressed: Do I really believe
that it is God that is doing, God that is acting? Or is the
revelatory experience of which I speak something simply
that men do by themselves and then postulate the acting
God as an explanation? It seems to me that this is an
inappropriate way to pose the question. Of course I believe that God acted on Sinai and in the history of Israel

and at Calvary and Easter. I believe that God acts in all human events and that he acted in a unique way in the dramatic religious encounters. Do I believe that God really spoke? If one means by this do I believe that he spoke the way he was depicted as doing in the movie *The Ten Commandments*, the answer is, obviously, no. If I am asked if there was really a voice speaking on the mountain that people could hear, I would say maybe. I wasn't there and I don't know. If there was a voice, it was not the voice of God. God does not have a voice. It must have been a modification of the air waves that God produced for the purpose of communicating with people. Such an event would be marvelous indeed, and since I believe in an open universe I would not want to exclude the possibility of such an event; but I will assert that under normal circumstances that is not the way God works. Indeed, which is more marvelous—a God who works through creating modifications in the air waves or a God who works through the growth of human insight and understanding?

In other words, I cannot accept a divorce between God's working and the growth of human insight and understanding. What occurred in the experience that Sinai symbolizes was a fantastic leap forward in human insight, and I think that such a leap is infinitely more impressive and dramatic than voices coming from a cloud on a mountaintop.

In any event, on Sinai, God worked and man worked. They worked together, and the result was an extraordinary religious event. Attempts to explain how the event occurred are much less important than the recognition that it did indeed occur.

CHAPTER 2

THE RELIGIOUS BACKGROUND

There are two problems that must be faced if we are to come to grips with the religious challenge presented in the nineteenth and twentieth chapters of the book of Exodus. First of all, we must rid ourselves completely of the notion that the Israelite religion emerged in an instant, fully developed and distinct from the religious and cultural currents which swirled around the ancient Middle East. The cult of Yahweh is unique. Nothing even remotely like it is found anywhere else in ancient times; but the uniqueness comes not from the development of totally new religious material but rather from the organization of existing religious material around a decisively new insight. There were unquestionably certain specific events which had a major impact on the development of the insight (Sinai was certainly one of those events), but the full development of new insight and the rearrangement of existing religious material was the work of years, probably centuries, and with periodic backslidings.

Furthermore, while some individuals, such as the historic Moses, unquestionably played a critical role in the development of the religious insight (how much of a role is difficult to tell from our vantage point), the evolution of the Israelite religion involved a fundamental shift in world view among a whole community of people, espe-

cially among its principal religious leaders. The Israelite
insight, then, was both individual and collective, the work
in part of extraordinarily gifted religious leaders and in
part of an anonymous but vigorous community.

Not so long ago, comparisons between the Old Testament documents and other ancient Middle Eastern religious documents were viewed by both believers and
non-believers as a threat to the uniqueness of the revelation reported in the Old Testament. Even today, many
Catholics, both priests and laity, are profoundly uneasy
when they hear comparisons between the Genesis creation myth and the Babylonian creation myth. But in the
world of serious biblical scholarship the terms of the
issue have been changed, for it is clear that however
much the Israelites may have borrowed material from the
religious environment in which they lived, they transformed it to suit their own particular understanding of
how the world began, an understanding whose uniqueness becomes even more apparent when compared with
others who used similar mythological symbols.

If one assumes that the Israelite religious insight
emerged over time, not merely as the result of individual
effort but as the result of the growth of collective belief,
then the tools of comparative religion are no longer a
threat to our understanding of the uniqueness of the
faith of Israel. They become a positive help. Indeed, it is
only when we come to grips with the basic questions
which the religious insight of Israel purports to answer
that we can understand how unique the Israelites' response was.

The other problem, in some ways exactly the opposite of
the first one, is the difficulty we have in trying to respect
the mythopoetic approach to religion. In our very rational
and cognitive age we tend to distinguish between history
and legend; the former we take to be true and the latter
to be false. Myths are not history, therefore they are

legend, and therefore they are false. Of course our own age is not without its legends and its myths, but most of us refuse to face the fact that mythmaking is part of the human condition, as much now as it was in the Middle East of the thirteenth century B.C.

The Israelites broke decisively with the nature myths that pervaded the world in which they lived and replaced them with the Sinai myth. It was an enormous leap forward in human religious understanding, but it neither abolished the mythopoetic approach to religion nor dispensed completely with the symbolic components of natural mythology.

Ancient man was aware that he lived in a world in which there were great "powers." He was aware of the cycle of life and death, of fertility and reproduction, of planting, growth, and harvest. He knew that the sun and the moon and the stars changed their position in the heavens. He realized the immense constraints that family, clan, and tribe imposed on his behavior. If he was Egyptian, he was awed by the rise and fall of the mighty Nile, which dominated every aspect of his life. He knew that sexuality was a force within him that was terribly difficult to restrain. He knew that there was thunder, lightning, storms, and drought; volcanoes, earthquakes, and eclipses. Most fundamental of all, he perceived around him a struggle between order and chaos. He understood the routine systems of both nature and human society, but he also perceived that these could be disrupted: in nature by the tremendous force of natural phenomena gone wild, in society by internal conflict or external invasion. There were, unquestionably, orderly routines in the world, but there was also constant disruption. There were powers of order and powers of chaos. Ancient man wondered (at least some of them) how it came to be that the world was.

We may have grown more skillful at formulating these

questions in abstract and theoretical ways, but we deceive ourselves if we think the questions are any less important to us than they were to our ancient ancestors or that our answers produce any more certainty than those of three and four millennia ago. The basic differences between us and our ancestors is that we use a different language to describe our experience of the "powers" which impose themselves on our lives. In the words of Jay G. Williams:

> The polytheistic mythologizer, then, simply sought to describe the variety of powers which affect man. He was not just a superstitious man purveying silly stories about imagined deities. Rather he was seeking to describe as concretely and as carefully as possible the powers which actually exerted influence over the lives of human beings.[1]

Williams continues to describe the mythologizer:

> He does not try to speculate about what the world is like apart from man. He develops no abstract notions about being and becoming or about atoms and the void, but instead, through the medium of poetry, tries to express the impact which the various powers of the universe make upon man, how they confront man, and how they are related one to another. The scientist may examine the meteorological causes of the sudden storm. The philosopher may search for principles for understanding change. But the mythologizer simply describes how the storm confronts man concretely and directly.[2]

In other words, myth is truth told not abstractly but concretely. The mythmaker may be a poet but he is not a superstitious fool; he has chosen to grapple with reality

[1] Jay G. Williams, *Ten Words of Freedom: An Introduction to the Faith of Israel.* Philadelphia: Fortress Press, 1971, p. 32.
[2] Ibid., p. 33.

with a story rather than a schematic proposition. Ancient man's way of telling the truth was to become emotionally and poetically involved in it.

Man the mythmaker is trying to come to terms with the problem that man the scientist tries—perhaps unsuccessfully—to declare insoluble, for ancient man was puzzled by the greatest mystery of all: the problem of human existence. In Paul Ricoeur's words:

> . . . Still more fundamentally, the myth tries to get at the enigma of human existence, namely, the discordance between fundamental reality—state of innocence, status of a creature, essential being—and the actual modality of man, as defiled, sinful, guilty. The myth accounts for this transition by means of a narration. But it is a narration precisely because there is no deduction, no logical transition, between the fundamental reality of man and his present existence, between his ontological status as a being created good and destined for happiness and his existential or historical status, experienced under the sign of alienation. Thus the myth has an ontological bearing: it points to the relation—that is to say, both the leap and the passage, the cut and the suture—between the essential being of man and his historical existence.[3]

The myth, then, is a comprehensive view of reality. It explains it, interprets it, provides the ritual by which man may maintain his contact with it, and even conveys certain very concrete notions about how reality is to be used to facilitate mankind's life and comfort. The men who created the myths and lived by them were not superstitious, foolish savages. They were not our predecessors in the evolutionary process. Intellectually, their style was different from ours—at least when we engage in abstract,

[3] Paul Ricoeur, *The Symbolism of Evil*. Translated by Emerson Buchanan. Boston: Beacon Press, 1967, p. 163, paperback.

objective science. But even science as practiced by men like Claude Lévi-Strauss and his colleagues seems to be in the process of discovering that mythopoesis as thought and expression may be indispensable in any comprehensive and adequate system of human knowledge.

The most obvious place to look for influences on the formation of the Israelite mythology is Egypt, whence escaped some of the Hebrew tribes who later settled in Palestine and integrated both the Exodus and the Sinai experience into their religious symbol system. The most powerful factor in the life of the Egyptians was the Nile River. The regular rise and fall of the Nile flood made possible the development of the longest single culture in the history of the human race. R. A. F. MacKenzie summarizes the fundamentally optimistic religion of the Egyptians:

> Life in the Nile Valley was a good life, and any change must be for the worse. History had no real meaning for them; existence was fixed in an unchanging rhythm of natural forces, to which they were well adjusted and which seemed incapable of improvement. There is a Christian formula which, applied strictly to the welfare of man and his harmony with the cosmos, rather neatly expresses the Egyptian outlook and hope: "As it was in the beginning, is now, and ever shall be, world without end." That was the business of the gods. Let them see to it that the Nile flowed regularly through the land, that it punctually and adequately rose in flood each summer, that the crops were abundant, that the north wind continued to blow, that the sun-god in particular made his daily majestic progress from east to west across the sky. Then the Egyptian knew that the gods were in their heaven, all was right with the world.[4]

[4] R. A. F. MacKenzie, S.J., *Faith and History in the Old Testament.* Minneapolis: University of Minnesota Press, 1963, p. 11.

Egyptian religion, then, was essentially a fertility cult; and the gods, whose names changed at different times in Egypt's history, basically guaranteed the annual flow of the Nile and the annual fruit of the field. In the century before the Hebrews fled from Egypt, there was an attempt on the part of the heretic king, Ikhnaton,[5] to establish a kind of monotheistic worship of the solar disk, Aten. There was much that was beautiful in the solar cult, as the following stanza from an Egyptian hymn makes clear:

> O creator of what the earth brings forth, Khnum and Amun of mankind! . . .
> Excellent mother of gods and man, good creator who takes the greatest pains with his innumerable creatures. . . .
> He who reaches the ends of the lands every day and beholds those who walk there. . . .
> Every land adores him at his rising every day, in order to praise him.[6]

But the cult of Aten did not last very long. Apparently it was a rather precious intellectual development presided over by a royal family whose sexual ethics were dubious (Nefretete was apparently Ikhnaton's half sister. His nephew and successor, Tut-ankh-amun, married his own youngest daughter. However, since he suffered from

[5] W. F. Albright makes it clear that the king himself was probably incapable of effecting the artistic and religious innovations attributed to him. Anatomical studies of his mummy show that he was physically deformed and underdeveloped in such a way that his emotional and intellectual growth was very likely stunted. Perhaps his mother, Queen Teye, his wife, Nefretete (whose lovely face still haunts us), or some other favorite was the guiding force during his reign. (See William Foxwell Albright, *From the Stone Age to Christianity*. Baltimore: Johns Hopkins Press, 1940, pp. 164–65.)

[6] Albright, op. cit., p. 166.

the same physical deformities as his predecessor, he was probably impotent, so his daughters' paternity is in some doubt.) Certainly, the new cult never penetrated to the masses or even to the priests and scribes. It deteriorated rapidly and was thrust aside with the accession of Rameses I and a new dynasty.

Some of the Israelite tribes were undoubtedly in Egypt at the time of the rise and fall of the Aten heresy. If we assume that there is some historical truth in the legends of Moses' early life, he certainly would have had some access to the theories of Egyptian solar monotheism. Even apart from this, it is unlikely that the Israelites could have lived in Egypt without knowing the official religion of the land despite its limited acceptance. If one wishes to find origins of monotheism in the religious environment of the Israelites, one can also discover such beginnings in their own Semitic tradition.

It may be difficult to document the extent of Egyptian influence on the Israelite religion, but there is no difficulty in tracing Babylonian imagery. In the famous story of Enuma Elish we have the Babylonian myth that explains the struggle between order and chaos in the universe. Marduk, the great Babylonian hero god, destroys the female sea monster, Tiamet, or "chaos." Out of the darkness of the monster he produces the orderly world. In the cosmogony of Mesopotamia, a god fights a battle over the powers of chaos and conquers them.

There can be no question that traces of this cosmogony can be found in the Old Testament. For example, in Psalm 89:8–11:

Yahweh of hosts, who is like you?
Your power and your faithfulness are your attendants.
You who rule over the raging of the sea,
when its waves rise you subdue them;

you who crushed Rahab like a corpse,
  with your strong arm scattered your enemies;
to you belong both sky and earth;
  the world and its contents, you have established them.

And in Isaiah 51:9–10, Yahweh is pictured as destroying the monster and providing order in the world just as Marduk did:

> Awake, awake, put on strength,
>   arm of Yahweh!
> Awake, as in the days of old,
>   the generations of ancient time.
> Was it not you that mangled Rahab,
>   that pierced the sea monster?
> Was it not you that dried up the sea,
>   the waters of the great Deep;
> that made the depths of the sea a pathway
>   for the redeemed to cross by?

Since this book is not primarily concerned with the Israelite creation story, there is no need to emphasize the obvious differences between Marduk's fighting the battle against chaos and ordering a preexistent reality and Yahweh calmly and effortlessly by a mere word bringing the whole of reality into being. Father R. A. F. MacKenzie summarizes the very considerable literature which has emphasized the different substance of the Babylonian myth and the Israelite myth.

> The language, the conventions, the symbols belong to a fixed and familiar genre, which owes most to the myths of Babylonia. In no other terms could a cosmogony or anthropogony be acceptable or comprehensible to the mentality of early Israel. It had to tell a story; it had to embody its teaching in such images as a wonderful garden, a talking snake, a magic tree.

Secondly, no ancient literature offers any parallel to the profundity, the penetration, with which psychological and theological truths are here so plastically expressed. They all depend on the central figure of the story, who is neither the Man nor the Woman, still less the Snake, but the Creator-God himself. No explanation is attempted of his origin; he is there, given existence; the question is only to explain the origin of his creatures. He does not need them; but he creates them and then lavishes on them his benefactions. The only return he expects from them, and the only one they can give him, is their personal loyalty, their acknowledgment of the truth that they are his. When they deplorably fail in this acknowledgment, and attempt to dispense with him—when they break the covenant of loyalty and gratitude—their punishment is less than they deserve, is tempered with indulgent mercy, and does not completely separate them from him.[7]

The authors of the two versions of the creation with which the book of Genesis begins use some of the imagery of the ancient Middle Eastern environment in which they found themselves, but they put the imagery to entirely different purposes. The Yahweh the Israelites knew in the Sinai experience did not have to fight any battles with monsters. He created the universe; it was all his; and he ordered it to suit his own good pleasure. Marduk is more than a power, perhaps; he had something of a personality, though Father MacKenzie says that it was feebly developed. In MacKenzie's words, "He never issued forth as a complete personality, never stepped out of his function as patron and personification of the city, never really became more than a heavenly symbol of the earthly primacy of Babylon."[8] Yahweh has a personality that is all his own.

[7] MacKenzie, op. cit., p. 55.
[8] Ibid., p. 17.

If one turns from the Babylonian to the Canaanite predecessors of the Israelites, one finds four different manifestations of divinity that are worth considering in our search to understand whence came Yahweh. First, there was in all likelihood some sort of vague "high god" lurking behind the pantheon of lesser deities. In Egypt, Babylonia, Greece, and virtually all of the other ancient kingdoms there loomed a high god in the background, but he was not important. Among the ancient Semite tribes, they were apparently ignored, probably because like the Greek Kronos they had become irrelevant. There is no record of any cult of the high god. One supposes that in any religion where there is some kind of tradition of a high god, there is the potential for monotheism, but if that god exercises no direct power in the world, the potential rarely becomes realized. There is, after all, no reason for dealing with a god who does not exercise power on earth and is incapable of responding to worship. Yahweh is a high god in the sense that he reigns over all the other gods, but he did not remain aloof. Quite the contrary, there were times when Israel found him altogether too much involved.

The ancestors of the Hebrews were devoted to fertility cults. The reproduction of their animals and, in a later age, the harvest of their fields were what kept them alive. William Foxwell Albright describes for us the fierceness of the Canaanite fertility worship:

> Goddesses of fertility play a much greater role among the Canaanites than they do among any other ancient people. The two dominant figures are Astarte and Anath, who are called in an Egyptian text of the New Empire "the great goddesses who conceive but do not bear," i.e., who are always virginal but who are none the less fruitful. . . . Another dominant characteristic of the Canaanite god-

desses in question was their savagery. In Egyptian
sources Astarte and Anath are preeminently god-
desses of war; a favorite type of representation
shows the naked goddess astride a galloping horse
and brandishing a weapon in her right hand. In a
fragment of the Baal epic . . . , Anath appears as
incredibly sanguinary. For a reason not yet known
she massacres mankind, young and old, from the
sea-coast to the rising of the sun, causing heads and
hands to fly in all directions. Then she ties heads to
her back, hands to her girdle, and wades up to her
knees—yes, up to her throat—in human gore. The
favorite animals of the Canaanite goddess were the
lion, because of its ferocity, and the serpent and
dove, because of their reputed fecundity.[9]

There are obvious traces of the fertility cult in the
Israelite religion. As we shall see later on, sexuality is at
the very core of the Israelite religion. The Feast of the
Paschal Lamb, originally in a pastoral context, and the
Feast of the Unleavened Bread, originally agricultural
(both combined later to become the Passover), were in
ancient times fertility rites marking the coming of spring.
It was no accident that the two feasts were converted
into a celebration of the covenant Yahweh made with his
people, a covenant which was viewed as a symbolic marriage from which all life was to come. The power of
fertility, then, was seen to be Yahweh's power and a
manifestation of Yahweh's love.

Walter Harrelson describes how the Israelite religion
took the themes and the symbols of fertility worship and
transformed them completely to be utilized by the Israelites' new religious insight.

Since Yahweh ruled alone as God, there was no
place for a goddess as his consort. The motif of

[9] Albright, op. cit., pp. 177–78.

fertility, prominent as it is in the Old Testament, seems to have been rigorously curtailed in the official cult of Israel. But the sacred marriage of god and goddess, symbolically represented through acts of sacred prostitution at the shrines and vividly portrayed in the ritual accompanying the New Year's Day acts outside Israel, was one of the most significant cultic acts of the festival. The power of man and beast to produce progeny was renewed and restored through such ritual acts. In no other respect is the Israelite cultus more sharply to be distinguished from the cultus of her neighbors than in the way in which fertility is dealt with. While we have evidence in the Song of Songs and in a few other biblical references for sacred prostitution and for fertility rites at the various shrines, such evidence can best be accounted for by the assumption that various groups at different times brought into Israelite worship this prominent element in the worship of Israel's neighbors. The official Yahwistic cult probably did not allow for such practices.

The theologians of ancient Israel came to understand Yahweh to be the creator of all fertility, providing within the natural order for a continuing appearance of life. It was Yahweh who at the time of creation had provided plants that produced their own seed, and animals and men who could procreate. The mystery of fertility was not eliminated, but the ritual acts and mythological explanations of those acts were slowly demythologized and fertility was drained of much of its numinous power in this way. God's good earth teemed with the power to produce living plants. On this good earth, means were provided for the birth and sustenance of animals and men.

Fertility was related to the history of Yahweh's salvation also. The prophet Hosea depicted Israel as the bride of Yahweh, but this bridal imagery was connected with the covenant made between God and people (Hosea 2), a covenant once made in the wilderness and thenceforth binding upon all the people. The Deuteronomistic historian was bitter in his opposition to the practices associated with fertility (Deuteronomy 23:17–18). But this historian and the tradition out of which he came saw in Yahweh's promise of a good land, flowing with milk and honey, rich in all the goods that made life full and complete, clear indication of Yahweh's control over the powers of fertility. This historian too, in his way, demythologized the mystery of fertility, relating it directly to the promise of Yahweh made to the forefathers, a promise in process of fulfillment, awaiting the End appointed by Yahweh when the entire earth would be transformed into a veritable paradise.[10]

Another Semite manifestation of the divinity was the tribal god, the deity whose particular responsibility and concern was with a given tribe. For the Semitic tribes this god (who frequently doubled as the male fertility principle) was thought of as living on a high mountain. The patriarchs of Israel knew this god as El Shaddai, the God of the Mountain or, as we suggested earlier in this book, the God of the Fruitful Mountain. This mountain deity is also a storm god, vaguely related to the Accadian Amurru, that is, the Western One, the god who is responsible for the storms in the west. The God of the Mountain, then, was responsible for fertility, the weather, and for protecting the tribe.

But the most important of all the Semite deities was the personal god of a man and his family. In Albright's words: ". . . the Hebrews, like their nomadic Semitic forefathers, possessed a very keen sense of the relationship between a patriarchal group (clan or family) and deity,

[10] Walter Harrelson, *From Fertility Cult to Worship.* Garden City, New York: Doubleday Anchor Books, 1970, pp. 54–55.

who was therefore an actual member of the clan and could be addressed by a mortal kinsman as 'father, brother,' and even as 'kindred.'"[11]

One did not get involved in such intimate relationships with Aten or Amon-Re or Marduk or Astarte or even with El Shaddai. The personal god of the family was different; he was someone you could talk to and understand. In the Genesis records we have indications of the various family gods: the Shield of Abraham, the Fear of Isaac (or maybe the word means the Kinsman of Isaac), and the Mighty One of Jacob. These were deities that were in some sense distinct from El Shaddai and were combined in later Israelite tradition to become the "God of the fathers." Since they didn't have a place of their own, the Semitic tribes were perhaps more inclined to develop a cult of the family god. After all, El Shaddai was on his mountaintop (wherever that was) and when you were a long way from the mountain, he might be interested no longer. The only god available, then, to fall back on was the one who was already a member of the family. Albright describes the two religious conceptions of the early Hebrews (both of which were characteristic of their environment) as follows:

1. a dynamistic belief in an undefined but real blood relationship between a family or clan and its god(s);
2. a recognition of the right of an independent man or founder of a clan to choose his own personal god, with whom he is expected to enter into a kind of contractual relationship. In combination, these ideas must have led to a form of tribal religion where both the collective and personal aspects of deity were present, the former in tribal acts of religious nature and the latter in individual worship.[12]

[11] Albright, op. cit., pp. 186–87.
[12] Ibid., p. 189.

What the Sinai insight involved was the recognition that El Shaddai and the God of the fathers were really the same God, the ruler of fertility and natural powers but also a close personal friend. Yahweh is, of course, more than just a combination of El Shaddai and the God of the fathers. But it seems reasonable to guess that the insight which combined these two manifestations of the deity was the first movement in the religious quantum leap that produced the notion of Yahweh, which we shall explore in the rest of this book.

Two other elements of the pre-Sinai tradition deserve mention. The first is the religious idea of "promise," which the interpreters of the Sinai experience would develop into a theology of "covenant." It is generally agreed that the verses in Deuteronomy 26:5–9 represent one of the most ancient texts of the Israelite tradition (notice, for example, that there is no reference to Sinai in the brief kerygma):

Then, in the sight of Yahweh your God, you must make this pronouncement:

"My father was a wandering Aramaean. He went down into Egypt to find refuge there, few in numbers; but there he became a nation, great, mighty, and strong. The Egyptians ill-treated us, they gave us no peace and inflicted harsh slavery on us. But we called on Yahweh the God of our fathers. Yahweh heard our voice and saw our misery, our toil and our oppression; and Yahweh brought us out of Egypt with mighty hand and outstretched arm, with great terror, and with signs and wonders. He brought us here and gave us this land, a land where milk and honey flow.[13]

There is in this text only a dim implication of a promise from Yahweh; that notion will be developed and become

[13] Deuteronomy 26:5–9, *The Jerusalem Bible*. Garden City, New York: Doubleday, 1966.

central in the Hebrew people's reflection on their own experiences. In Gerhard von Rad's description of the developments:

> ... the era of the patriarchs as a whole is under-
> stood as the time of the promise, as an elaborate
> preparatory arrangement for the creation of the peo-
> ple of God and for its life. What is new in this view
> is not the use of the idea of the promise in itself—
> ... the promise of a land and of children already
> formed a part of the oldest traditions deriving from
> the patriarchal age. What is new is rather the
> theological employment of this twofold promise as a
> word of God which set in motion the whole of the
> saving history down to the conquest under Joshua.
> Behind this conception lies a prolonged and insistent
> reflection upon herself on Israel's part. The Israel
> which had become conscious of her peculiarity now
> felt the need to visualize how she came into being.
> Thus, there lies behind the patriarchal history in the
> Hexateuch a mighty amazement at the far-reaching
> preparations which Jahweh had made to summon
> Israel into being.[14]

Finally, the contemporary Israeli scholar Yehezkel Kaufmann points out that Moses may very well have been a *kāhin*, an Arab pagan prophet, frequently part of a family of seers. Moses, Aaron, and Miriam were all spokesmen of God. Kaufmann illustrates the *kāhin*ic nature of Moses by noting the similarity between the roles played by him and Mohammed among their respective peoples:

> Like the *kāhin*, Moses is not connected with an
> established temple or cult. Whether Moses was ever
> himself a *kāhin* or not, he seems to have grown up
> among a family of such seers, and this surely affected

[14] Gerhard von Rad, *Old Testament Theology*, Vol. I. New York: Harper & Brothers, 1962, p. 170.

him. The ancient Hebrew *kāhin*-clairvoyant was the
social type that served as the vehicle of his appearance as prophet and leader. The case of Mohammed
in later times is an instructive parallel. Mohammed
was not an actual *kāhin*, but his visions and poetic
expression grew out of the soil of *kāhin* prophecy.
At first Mohammed feared that he was nothing but a
possessed *kāhin*, until he became convinced that an
angel was speaking with him. If the content of his
prophecy was not *kāhin*ic, its form was, and his influence and acceptance among his contemporaries
were founded on the current belief in *kāhin* prophecy. Similarly, the new message of Moses clothed
itself in a form familiar to the people of those times.
That a divine spirit revealed itself to a lonely seer
was not an incredible thing; that this man should
become a leader of his people was also not unheard
of. And, since the ancient Hebrew seer was not
bound by a specific cult or temple, Moses enjoyed
the freedom necessary for the expression of a new
idea. To this seer, however, there appeared not a
familiar spirit but a supernal, omnipotent God. Moses
returned to his people not a clairvoyant, but a messenger of God.[15]

Moses' experience of God in the burning bush
and the various ecstatic or quasi-ecstatic experiences of
the journey through the desert can be seen as having
some correspondence to the experiences of the ecstatic
prophets of the ancient Semitic tribes. Moses was both
the last and the first: He was the last Hebrew *kāhin* or
seer and the first messenger of God. It was Moses who
told the disparate Israelite tribes the name Yahweh, and
it was he who united them under that name with Yahweh's
promise of redemption.

[15] Yehezkel Kaufmann, *The Religion of Israel*. Translated and
abridged by Moshe Greenberg. Chicago: The University of Chicago
Press, 1960, pp. 227–28.

It is easy for us to feel greatly superior to all the ancient threads of cult and paganism that may be traced in early descriptions of Yahweh. We do not need a god to explain fertility or the weather, or to protect us against the vagaries of wandering in the desert; our family lives are quite secure without postulating a deity lurking on the hearth or in the attic. The powers of the universe no longer threaten us; on the contrary, we control many of them and are hopeful that someday we will control everything. We don't need El Shaddai or Marduk or Amon-Re or Aten or any other of those weird and rather frightening characters. And while there is a certain charm in the Shield of Abraham or the Kinsman of Isaac, we don't see them as being much more relevant than patron saints or guardian angels. God may or may not be dead, but the gods long ago ceased to have any meaning for human life. Man, as Dietrich Bonhoeffer told us, has come of age, and gods are not only no longer required, they must be dismissed as a threat to man's freedom and his full humanity.

Well, maybe. But for all our wisdom, it could be questioned whether we have any more satisfactory ultimate answers to the mystery of human life and death than our nomadic predecessors did. Nor can we explain human sinfulness, the struggle between order and chaos, the tragedy and comedy, the glory and the disappointment of human existence any better than they could. And it turns out that our immense powers over the physical world frequently serve to pollute and destroy that world, and thus, eventually, to destroy us. Human existence may be a bit longer and somewhat less uncertain than it was in the thirteenth century before Christ, but it is still a chancy, problematic affair. If we no longer explain thunderstorms by such mythological creatures as giant vultures, we still are content to create mythological monsters like the "Establishment" to provide simple and comprehensible explanations for the problems that beset us. We desperately look for some functional equivalent of Marduk (preferably possessing Consciousness III) to slay the great monster Establishment, establish order, and make America green again.

Our sophisticated explanations of the weather, the fertility cycle, and the progression of the stars across the heavens do not provide either answers for the most fundamental questions man can ask or ethical norms which enable us to live with each other in peace and harmony and constructive respect for our physical world. That we are religiously superior to the Babylonians or the Egyptians or the Canaanites or the pre-Sinai Semites is not immediately obvious. We may know more than those ancient peoples about many things and we may have a higher degree of ethical sensitivity, but those problems which baffled them also baffle us, and man's tragic inability to live in peace with his fellows was surely no more destructive in their time than it is in ours.

Perhaps, after all, we ought to journey to the foot of Sinai to see what is going on there and to learn what this Yahweh god has to offer.

CHAPTER 3

COVENANT

The covenant symbol contains the basic theme of the Sinai revelation and of the Jewish religion. By the covenant symbol Israel claimed a unique relation with the deity. In other ancient religions God was identified either with nature or with the society that worshiped him, but for Israel the relationship with God was the result of a positive action on the part of Yahweh himself. It was an action that demanded a positive response from Israel. It was not part of the necessary conditions of human existence, either natural or social, but was rather a relationship that was free on both sides.

The emergence of the covenant symbol may well be the most dramatic change in the whole history of human religions. Even the later cross and resurrection symbolism of Christianity are, in the final analysis, merely a further development of the covenant symbolism. Most of us, unfortunately, are so familiar with the idea of covenant (in the bad translation of the word into English as "testament") that we take the symbol for granted. It is part of our religious environment, and we rarely pause to realize how striking and dramatic it is. God has made a covenant with us? Well, of course, so what else is new?

Undoubtedly, the idea of a covenant between God and his people had its origins in the pre-Sinai tradition of a "promise" made by the God of the fathers. The covenant symbol could be used to reorder and reinterpret the pre-Sinai traditions. But a covenant, as we shall shortly see, is far more than a promise, and Yahweh on Sinai is far more than a Kinsman of Isaac. A covenant (the Hebrew word is *berith*) was very much part of the social life of the ancient desert countries. It was a treaty, a pact, an agreement that established a permanent relationship between those who entered the agreement. The parties to the relationship could be two individuals, two families, or two peoples. Covenants between kings, acting either as individuals or for their collective units, were especially frequent. The result of a covenant was an extremely close bond, indeed, one equivalent to the closest natural bond. Those who entered the covenant bound themselves under penalty of curse and destruction to fidelity and to assistance. There was a special word to describe responsibilities resulting from a covenant relationship; the word in Hebrew is *hesed*. We shall see more of this word in a later chapter. Father R. A. F. MacKenzie's comments on it are appropriate at this point: "Though impossible to translate adequately, since it combines the ideas of love, loyalty, and ready action, . . . it may be rendered 'loving kindness,' or perhaps better 'covenant love.'"[1] God and Israel had made a pact freely entered into on both sides, which bound God and the people to one another in a most intimate sort of relationship, one in which he committed himself to act toward his people with loving kindness.

There are other symbols in the Old Testament which attempt to cope with Israel's experience of Yahweh. It is described as a father-son relationship, as a shepherd-flock relationship, as a king-subject relationship, a relationship among kin, and, especially, as a marriage relationship.

[1] MacKenzie, *Faith and History in the Old Testament*, op. cit., p. 38.

However, it is generally agreed now that a covenant symbol is the basic one and the key to all the others, though as we shall see in a subsequent chapter, the very language used to describe the covenant makes the marriage symbol almost immediately obvious.

The last four books of the Pentateuch are, in effect, simply variations on the theme of the covenant between Yahweh and his people. There is some question as to exactly when the theme became central in Israelite religion. Men had a religious experience and then attempted to describe that experience to themselves and others through the use of whatever symbols were available to them, however inadequate those symbols might be. The apostles, for example, had a profound religious experience of Jesus both before and especially after Easter. Jesus himself was apparently rather reluctant to use any titles or labels. It was sufficient for him that he announced the kingdom of God, the kingdom of *his* Father. But the apostles had to describe and explain the experience, and so they fell back necessarily on the vocabulary of their time and spoke of "Messiah," "Son of Man," "Prophet," and "King." Similarly, the Israelites had an experience of Yahweh and found in the covenant customs of their time a symbol which told them and then others what the experience had meant. It is not easy for us to reconstruct the nature of that experience, but it had something to do with the collection of disparate and wandering tribes suddenly becoming conscious that they were a people, that God had made them a people, hence, inevitably, *his* people. They were a disorganized assemblage of nomadic tribes and suddenly they were one, not under any earthly ruler, only under Yahweh. Yahweh had intervened and made them a people; this intervention seemed to correspond to other agreements that kings made with their peoples, and so, for them, it was a covenant.

We wonder, of course, how long it took for this sense of

union as a people to become translated into the covenant symbolism. Most scholars at this time are ready to concede that the covenant symbolism probably emerged in the desert even before the invasion and occupation of Palestine. Hence, the symbol probably came into being rather quickly after the event. The tradition with which we are especially concerned as recorded in the nineteenth and twentieth chapters of Exodus probably dates, though hardly in its present form, to the desert experience. The account of the covenant in the twenty-fourth chapter of the book of Joshua is more likely to be a version with its origin to be found in Palestine after the occupation.

The covenant, according to George E. Mendenhall, is a "suzerainty treaty by which a great king bound his vassals to faithfulness and obedience to himself."[2] Mendenhall traces evidence of the existence of covenants to Babylonia, Assyria, the Hittite Empire, and Egypt. There are generally six components in the Hittite covenant treaties that are available to us (Hittite covenant treaties are the only ones available of those ancient cultures):[3]

1. The preamble, which names the king and gives his background.

2. The historical prologue, which sets forth the previous relationship between the parties—generally in an "I-Thou" form of address.

3. The conditions imposed upon those with whom the covenant is made. For example, the prohibition of other foreign relations, the maintenance of peace, military assistance, and confidence in the king.

4. The requirement that the treaty be deposited in the temple and that it be read to the people periodically.

[2] George E. Mendenhall, "Law and Covenant in Israel and the Ancient Near East," reprint from *The Biblical Archaeologist*, Vol. XVII, No. 2 (May 1954). Pittsburgh, Pennsylvania: The Biblical Colloquium, 1955, p. 26.

[3] Cf. Ibid., pp. 32–34.

5. A list of the gods who witness the treaty.

6. Curses and blessings for violation and fulfillment of the treaty.

In addition there are other factors involved which generally did not appear in the written form of the treaty: the formal oath of obedience, a solemn ceremony which accompanied the oath and its renewal, and, finally, a procedure for taking action against a rebellious or unfaithful partner of the covenant.

The various descriptions contained in the books of Exodus, Deuteronomy, and Joshua of the covenant between Yahweh and his people parallel rather closely the Hittite treaty forms. There is a preamble ("I am the Lord, thy God"), a historical prologue ("who brought you out of the land of Egypt"), a set of stipulations (Exodus 20, the Ten Commandments), and a ceremony of oath and commitment of the sort described in Exodus 24:4–8. There is no explicit statement of curses and blessings, though surely the first commandment of the Decalogue implies that it would be just as well not to anger the "impassioned" Yahweh. Nor is there a list of gods as witnesses, but of course Yahweh doesn't need any other gods to witness the covenant which he enters. Finally, while there is no description of a requirement for periodic reading or deposit in the temple, we do know that every seven years in Palestine there was a great ceremony at Shechem renewing the covenant; there is every reason to assume that the present text of chapters 19 and 20 of Exodus were part of that liturgy of covenant renewal.

The account, then, of the beginning of Israel's relationship with Yahweh was designed, in all likelihood explicitly and consciously, to parallel the treaties by which individuals and tribes constituted themselves a people together with their king.

But it would be a mistake for us to think that the covenant with Yahweh was like any other covenant that existed in the ancient Middle East. For if it were simply a treaty binding together a number of tribes under a new leader, the covenant would have been with Moses; he was the leader of the tribes. But Moses did not present himself as the overlord with whom the covenant was made. On the contrary, he was the go-between—humble, frightened, and not always reliable. It was no earthly leader Israel dealt with, and it was no brilliant monarch who forged them as a people. It was Yahweh, the Lord of Creation. The stipulations he makes are totally different from those of other suzerains. He is not concerned about military might and pledges of assistance in time of war. He does not need these things; he demands the fidelity of his people, a fidelity evidenced by their loyalty to him. Nor are the stipulations he imposes on his people complicated or rigorous, not, at least, in their most primitive form. Other than fidelity to him, he demands nothing in the way of specific action; he only forbids behavior which is inappropriate for a people who are his followers: They shall not lie or steal or commit adultery. The way they choose to respond to his love is left to their own free determination. In later years, these stipulations would be expanded into a complex legal system, imposing a vast number of obligations, which purported to measure the amount of response to Yahweh's commitment. There was considerable resistance to this development. Deuteronomy may well have been the last effort to resist the rigid formulation of obligations. As von Rad says, "Indeed, in reducing all the profusion of the commandments to the one fundamental commandment, to love God (Deut. VI:5), and in concerning itself so earnestly with the inner, the spiritual, meaning of the commandments, Deuteronomy rather looks like a last stand against the beginning of a legalisation."[4]

Even though Deuteronomy was a relatively late book in

[4] Von Rad, *Old Testament Theology*, Vol. I, op. cit., p. 201.

the Israelite religious tradition, there seems to be little
doubt that the command "Hear us, O Israel, the Lord is
our God, the Lord alone. You must love the Lord, your
God, with all your heart and with all your soul and with
all your mind" represents all the basic insight of the
ancient Sinai covenant far more adequately than all the
detailed legislation that later became part of "the Law."
On Sinai Yahweh stipulated that his people love him in
response to his love for them, and that was about all
that he demanded. The legalism that emerged in later
centuries was a manifestation of the apparently incurable
human tendency to deal with God by keeping rules rather
than by responding with love.

What the covenant symbol says, then, is that the God
of Moses is not a mountain spirit but a free agent and
Lord of the Universe. He can convert an outlawed shepherd like Moses into a prophet; he can turn an unorganized
group of slaves into a closely knit people. What is more,
he can make this people his people, whose mission it was
to bring his word to the non-covenant peoples. The whole
nation was a priestly nation because the whole nation was
called to bear witness to Yahweh's love. Israel was the
light, the priest, and the sacrificial victim offered for the
sins of all the people.

But the covenant was more than just a mystical event.
It was a structured relationship between God and man;
it was a record of the experience of a disorganized, disparate welter of tribes who were suddenly a people, and
who could think of no other explanation for the emergence
of their federation than the intervention of a proximate
and passionate God, deeply, one might say, desperately
involved in human affairs. He would use this people of
his for worldwide, cosmic purposes.

Just as their social and political bond had nothing to
do with royal families, religious hierarchies, and military
confederations, so the mission of the people had nothing

to do with flood control, defense, or the establishment of empires. The mission of Israel was to reveal Yahweh's love.

In form, then, the covenant was like other covenants, but in purpose, in content, and, above all, in origin it was completely different. Gerhard von Rad summarizes this use of the covenant theme to explain Israel and its history:

> Thus, in the final state of the Hexateuch, the following division of the traditional materials into periods emerges. God created the world and man. After the destruction of the corrupt human race by the Flood, God gave to a new human race laws for its self-preservation, and, in the covenant with Noah, guaranteed to it the outward continuance of the world and its orders. He then called Abraham, and in a covenant which he made with him, promised him a great posterity, a special relationship to God, and the land of Canaan. The first promise was fulfilled in Egypt, when the patriarchs grew into a people; the second was fulfilled at Sinai, when with a fresh covenant Israel received the regulations for her community life and her intercourse with God; and the third was fulfilled when under Joshua Israel took possession of the land of Canaan. Thus, by means of the covenant theology, the entire mass of the Hexateuchal traditions was set beneath a three fold arch of prophecy and fulfillment. Initially, there were only the patriarchs: they are not yet a people, they have not entered into the promised special relationship with God, nor do they possess a land. Then, from the patriarchs a people comes into being; but it is without the special relationship with the land. And finally, in what is perhaps really the most exciting period, Israel, which is entirely ordered in one direction only, that is towards Jahweh, towards the last promise, the land of Canaan.[5]

[5] Ibid., p. 135.

The covenant, both the reality and the symbol, would suffer many vicissitudes in the history of Israel; for Israel would not always remain loyal to Yahweh. Furthermore, at a later time in its history, the covenant was thought to exist not so much between Yahweh and the whole people as between Yahweh and the Davidic monarchy. In most classical prophets, there is no reference to covenant—even though the idea of Yahweh's love for his people was still of the highest importance to the prophets. But in Jeremiah and Ezekiel the idea of covenant returns, and now it is suffused with that which was only implicit in the book of Exodus—the symbolism of marriage.

Furthermore, the covenant was presumed to be between Yahweh and the whole people; salvation was a collective, not an individual matter. Only very slowly and gradually did the idea emerge that Yahweh also had a relationship with individuals. Nevertheless, despite failures in the practice and understanding of the covenant, it remained, at least implicitly, the central theme of Israelite religion. It is also, though in a different fashion, the central theme of the Christian religion.

What are we to make of this whole affair? A group of Semitic slaves escapes from Egypt. Some of their neighbors have a peculiar experience near a sacred mountain in the desert. They come together with other tribes around a desert oasis. There is no political unity and no one strong enough to become king. Out of the sheer necessity of maintaining some sort of peace with one another an amphictyony emerges, that is, a tribal confederation based on a common religious belief. The tribes discover that this religious belief, centered on one God, isolates them from neighboring cultures and forges them into one people. They occupy Palestine, and to maintain their unity in new circumstances, they periodically recommit themselves to the covenant. Later, their religious thinkers begin to use the covenant theme to interpret past traditions and to explicate a universal mission for this rather grab-bag collection of tribes now transformed into a self-conscious nation.

A collection of remarkable events, perhaps, certainly unique in the ancient world. One could understand why the experience of becoming a nation would be so astonishing to the disparate tribal collectivity, particularly when it was simply a belief in one common God which merged them. Obviously, it had to be a powerful God to accomplish such a feat. The experience of becoming a people through common worship forced the Israelite tribes to postulate a rather extraordinary God, who intervened in their affairs to accomplish a unity they were unable to accomplish themselves.

The random probability of political, social, economic, geographic, and cultural forces in the desert south of Palestine had produced a situation in which the development of new religious symbols was both necessary and inevitable. The event was remarkable, nonetheless; and some of the men in it must have been religious and political geniuses.

And so, having analyzed the emergence of Yahwism and having provided reasonable and plausible explanations for it, we sophisticated modern men think that we understand what happened, and we turn our faces from Sinai with the firm conviction that we need not take Yahweh very seriously.

It never occurs to us that the emergence of a brilliant and dramatic new religious insight out of a historical, social, and cultural experience might be more marvelous than Yahweh's personally engraving letters on stone tablets ever could be. Nor does it occur to us that Yahweh's promise to the patriarchs and to the Israelites that they would reveal his name to all nations has turned out to be a remarkably accurate one. Finally, we see no reason at all why after we have explained the social and cultural factors that produced Yahwism, it should also be necessary for us to ask the most fundamental religious question: Does the symbol of a God entering a treaty with his people tell us something about the nature of the Really Real that must be listened to and either accepted or rejected quite independently of our explanations of how this symbol came into being?

As we shall see in the subsequent chapters of this book, the Yahweh who appears on Sinai is far more than is required merely to hold a tribal confederation together. We learned moderns may persuade ourselves that we understand his origins and thereby we limit him by our categories, but unless we are the kind of men and women who believe that all reality can be contained in books in the library, we must still ask ourselves the question, what if Yahweh is real? What if the universe really is what the covenant symbolism tells us that it is? What if the Ground of Being, the fundamental creative principle, really does intervene in human events? What if he is a proximate and passionate God? What then?

To have explained more or less effectively the social and cultural origins of Yahwism does not provide answers to those questions. We may reject Yahweh because he is absurd and because the vision of reality which he symbolizes is much too good to be true. We may also dismiss him because a God who meddles in human affairs and converts a wandering collection of tribes into a people is an unworthy God. No God with any self-respect would bother with such affairs. (Hilaire Belloc says in his famous poem, "How odd/of God/to choose/the Jews." Such an oddity surely can't be a real God.)

Or we may choose to accept him. We may, to paraphrase slightly Schubert Ogden's comment about Jesus, say that any God who does not correspond to the covenant-making Yahweh is not a God worth believing in. But any response of acceptance requires an act of faith and commitment. Social and historical explanations, no matter how great the erudition in which they are rooted, will not provide sufficient grounds for a commitment of faith. The important question for faith is not how the Israelites came up with the notion that the deity is deeply involved in a love relationship with us; the important question is are we willing to commit our lives to the notion that basic Reality is loving? Anybody who thinks he can answer that question with historical or archaeological or cultural or scientific data simply doesn't know what he is talking about.

The fundamental insight of Israel is that God is *involved*. He is committed; he *cares* for his people. As we shall see later, he cares passionately for them. This insight so transcends the culture of the ancient Middle East, indeed, even the culture of our own time, that it still is literally incredible, literally too good to be true. It is rejected today or believed only weakly by those who profess it because its absurdity is too great for our cynical human intelligence.

There is, I think, more than just the notion that Yahweh is a God who *cares*. The Sinai symbolism tells us that he is a God who cannot help caring. He is involved because he has no choice but to be involved. I am certainly not denying the obvious fact that Yahweh is depicted as freely entering the covenant. Yet, once he has entered into it, he is portrayed as someone who is deeply concerned about its continuation. He does not need anything his people have to offer, but at the same time he desperately wants *them*. Francis Thompson's famous poem about God pursuing man like a hunting dog is grounded ultimately in the covenant symbolism. Yahweh *wants* his people. He is satisfied with nothing short of their whole devotion and their whole love. He demands their complete trust in him and will accept nothing less than that. Yahweh is not merely a God, not merely a Jewish God;

he is a pushy Jewish God who refuses to leave his people alone. The idea seems ridiculous if not blasphemous. Why should God push his way into our lives? Why should he elbow himself into our condition? Why can't he leave us alone? Why does he bother with our silly problems? Why should he have bothered with the problems of those illiterate and unattractive desert tribes of the thirteenth century B.C.?

An aloof desert god on the mountain, a warm and cozy family god to whom you could talk, a fertility goddess who guaranteed the continuation of the food production cycles—all of these are reasonable gods. So, too, is Marduk, who keeps chaos at bay, and the storm gods, who must be propitiated by magic. They behave the way gods ought to behave. They are independent, stern, aloof, cold. While sometimes they have all too human frailties, their emotions are not really anthropomorphic. They may, as in Greece, get involved with attractive individuals of the opposite sex, but they really don't care much about the human race. Such gods are easy to believe in and easy to reject. When many moderns reject Yahweh, they think it is that kind of god they are rejecting. We who are supposed to depend on the Yahwistic tradition have been so inept in proclaiming it that men can reject him, thinking that they are, after all, rejecting someone rather like Marduk or Amon-Re or Zeus or even El Shaddai. To accept or reject such a god is relatively simple, particularly since neither decision will have any impact on our lives. But to reject Yahweh means to turn one's back on the idea that love beats at the core of the universe. It means to reject the best news the human race has ever heard. On the other hand, to accept Yahweh—well, that means a radical and profound transformation of everything we do, because it means we can lead lives of trust and confidence. It is much better to explain how the Israelite tribes came up with the idea of Yahweh or to argue interminably about whether he really exists or not; for if we can occupy ourselves with these questions, we do not have to take seriously the challenge of a deity who says to us, "I am the Lord, your God, who have brought you out of the land of Egypt . . . an impassioned God, showing kindness to the thousands of generations of those who love me."

As far as we are concerned, it would be much better if that sort of God had remained on Sinai and kept his strange, pushy ideas to himself.

CHAPTER 4

PREPARATION

On the third new moon after the Israelites had
gone forth from the land of Egypt, on that very day,
they entered the wilderness of Sinai. Having jour-
neyed from Rephidim, they entered the wilderness of
Sinai and encamped in the wilderness. Israel encamped there in front of the mountain, and Moses
went up to God. The LORD called to him from the
mountain, saying, "Thus shall you say to the house
of Jacob and declare to the children of Israel: 'You
have seen what I did to the Egyptians, how I bore
you on eagles' wings and brought you to Me. Now
then, if you will obey Me faithfully and keep My
covenant, you shall be My treasured possession
among all the peoples. Indeed, all the earth is Mine,
but you shall be to Me a kingdom of priests and a
holy nation.' These are the words that you shall speak
to the children of Israel."

Moses came and summoned the elders of the people and put before them all the words that the
LORD had commanded him. All the people answered as one, saying, "All that the LORD has
spoken we will do!" And Moses brought back the
people's words to the LORD. And the LORD said to
Moses, "I will come to you in a thick cloud, in order
that the people may hear when I speak with you
and so trust you thereafter." Then Moses reported the

people's words to the LORD, and the LORD said to
Moses, "Go to the people and warn them to stay pure
today and tomorrow. Let them wash their clothes.
Let them be ready for the third day; for on the
third day the LORD will come down, in the sight
of all the people, on Mount Sinai. You shall set
bounds for the people round about, saying, 'Beware
of going up the mountain or touching the border of
it. Whoever touches the mountain shall be put to
death: no hand shall touch him, but he shall be either
stoned or pierced through; beast or man, he shall not
live.' When the ram's horn sounds a long blast, they
shall come up unto the mountain."

Moses came down from the mountain to the people and warned the people to stay pure, and they
washed their clothes. And he said to the people, "Be
ready for the third day: do not go near a woman."

On the third day, as morning dawned, there was
thunder, and lightning, and a dense cloud upon the
mountain, and a very loud blast of the horn; and all
the people who were in the camp trembled. Moses
led the people out of the camp toward God, and they
took their places at the foot of the mountain.

Now Mount Sinai was all in smoke, for the LORD
had come down upon it in fire; the smoke rose like
the smoke of a kiln, and the whole mountain trembled violently. The blare of the horn grew louder
and louder. As Moses spoke, God answered him in
thunder. The LORD came down upon Mount Sinai,
on the top of the mountain, and the LORD called
Moses to the top of the mountain and Moses went
up. The LORD said to Moses, "Go down, warn the
people not to break through to the LORD to gaze,
lest many of them perish. The priests also, who come
near the LORD, must purify themselves, lest the
LORD break out against them." But Moses said to
the LORD, "The people cannot come up to Mount
Sinai, for You warned us saying, 'Set bounds about
the mountain and sanctify it.'" So the LORD said

to him, "Go down, and come back together with Aaron; but let not the priests or the people break through to come up to the LORD, lest He break out against them." And Moses went down to the people and spoke to them. (The Torah, Exodus 19)

I suppose that most people who attended Catholic grammar school, high school, and college probably heard about the Ten Commandments at least once a year throughout the years of their education. It would be a safe wager that for practically all of us at no time in those sixteen years did we ever hear anything about Chapter 19 of the book of Exodus as a preparation for Chapter 20. Here were the ten rules God had laid down: no adultery, no bad thoughts, no lying, no stealing, no coveting (whatever in the world that was), go to Mass on Sunday (never mind that Sunday wasn't the sabbath), do what your parents, teachers, and pastor tell you to do, and, oh yes, don't use God's name irreverently, and don't fool around with spiritualistic séances under pain of excommunication.

If one assumes that the Decalogue is essentially an ethical code containing at least in embryonic form all the appropriate proscriptions of human behavior, then such an approach is perfectly valid. The rather bizarre events in Chapter 19 of Exodus—indeed, throughout the whole book—have nothing to do really with moral proscriptions. They are interesting accounts, filled with rather odd imagery; but since they don't tell us when "bad thoughts" turn from venial sins into mortal ones or how much work on Sunday violates the sabbath or how late you can come into Mass without having to hear it all over again, then there is nothing to be learned from Exodus about the meaning of the Ten Commandments.

In fact, however, the Ten Commandments are not basically an ethical code at all. In Gerhard von Rad's precise words, ". . . Israel certainly did not understand the Decalogue as an absolute moral law prescribing ethics: she rather recognised it as a revelation vouchsafed to her at a particular moment in her history, through which she was offered the saving gift of life."[1]

For many Catholics and, indeed, for many non-Catholic Christians, this notion is terribly difficult to accept. It involves a wrenching away from past preconceptions. All our lives we have believed that the Decalogue is the basic outline of a detailed code of moral behavior by which we earn life from God. Now we are told that that is not the way ancient Israel viewed it at all. It was rather an element in a saving gift that God offered to his people. The Decalogue is not an isolated moral code; it is part of a religious revelation. Our proper response to it is not so much to worry about keeping ethical rules as it is to believe in the gift of life that has been offered.

I am not suggesting that there is not an ethical component in the Sinai revelation, for there certainly is, though it is a very generalized one. The important point is that the component is a consequence of the covenant that Yahweh made with us; it is not the essence of that revelation. Yahweh did not appear on Sinai and say, "These are the rules of the game. You must keep them." He said, rather, "I am the Lord your God. I love you and you will be my people. Since you are my people and since you have responded to my love with faith, these are some of the things that you will not do." Thus, honoring one's parents and not killing, stealing, or committing adultery are consequences and evidences of the acceptance of Yahweh's love. They are not a set of conditions imposed on us for earning that love. We keep the Commandments not because Yahweh has told us we must but because he loves us. Insofar as the Decalogue has an ethical component, it is an ethic that follows from God's love for his people.

[1] Von Rad, *Old Testament Theology*, Vol. I, op. cit., pp. 194–95.

If our abstinence from murder, theft, adultery, and covetousness is not permeated by our faith in that love, then
it has nothing to do with the Yahweh who spoke to us
from Sinai.

I argued in my book *The Jesus Myth* that contemporary scripture scholarship, far from weakening religious
faith, makes the dimensions of that faith much clearer.
The interpretation that critical scholarship puts on chapters 19 and 20 of Exodus is a classic example of this point.
It was easy enough for us to pull the Ten Commandments
out of the religious context in which they are set and convert them into a detached ethical system when we didn't
understand what the context was. But now the scripture
scholars are quite certain that we have in chapters 19
and 20 (and at least segments of the subsequent chapters)
a liturgical text, part of a worship service. Taking the
Decalogue out of that text and trying to develop from
it a philosophy of human life makes no more sense than to
remove the Gloria from the Eucharistic liturgy and de-
ducing from it the essence of Christianity.

It is now generally agreed that in Israel during the
time of the judges, and indeed probably even after that
time, the Decalogue was read as the midpoint of the
solemn renewal of the covenant, a festival which occurred
every seven years at Shechem. As Gerhard von Rad says:

> If Israel at regular intervals celebrated the revelation
> at Sinai in the cult in such a way, we can in turn
> deduce from this how ardently she looked on this
> divine revelation as momentous. With this proclama-
> tion of the divine law something came about for her,
> and that not only in the so-called "spiritual sphere";
> rather did this conveyance to Jahweh have its con-
> sequences principally on the plane of concrete his-
> torical events. For in the cultic celebration Israel
> gave expression to the fact that the event which

took place at Sinai had an undiminished importance
for each age: it was renewed upon each succeeding
generation: it was for all of them "contemporary."[2]

The text that we have, then, in Exodus 19 and 20 is
part of a celebration of a momentous experience of God,
a celebration designed to re-create, so far as was possible,
the awe and wonder of that primal experience. It is an
experience of a righteous God, but his righteousness consists not so much in the punishment of sin as in the revelation of his loyalty and his community relationship
with Israel. In the renewal of the covenant Yahweh is
presented as asserting once more his *hesed*, his loving
care of his people. As von Rad puts it, "There is no terror
here, and no sighing, as if they were a burden, but only
thankfulness and praise."[3] The purpose, then, of the festival of the covenant renewal was to put to the children
of Israel once more the challenge of the past. Israel encounters Yahweh once again, and once again, it is forced
to a decision about life and death. As von Rad says,
"When Israel heard this utterance, she was put in a position from which there was no more going back."[4] Thus,
the texts of Exodus 19 and 20, as we have them, are not
so much a demand for moral integrity as they are a demand for faith. The renewal at Shechem was not an exercise in memory or an examination of conscience about
moral failings; it was rather a renewed challenge to faith.
The ceremony of which our text was a part did not ask
Israel in effect, do you commit sins? but, do you still
believe in Yahweh's love?

In this perspective the Commandments are but an outline, a Decalogue that, as von Rad says, "confines itself to

[2] Ibid., p. 193.
[3] Ibid., p. 196. Von Rad adds, "Israel only encountered the law
in its function as judge and destroyer at the time of the preaching
of the prophets" (p. 196).
[4] Ibid., p. 196.

a few basic negations; that is, it is content with, as it were, signposts on the margins of a wide sphere of life to which he who belongs to Jahweh has to give heed."[5] Von Rad continues:

> Within the sphere of life thus circumscribed by the commandments there lies a wide field of moral action which remains completely unregulated (after all, idolatry, murder, and adultery were not constant occurrences in Israel's everyday life). If then these commandments do not subject life in any way to a comprehensive normative law, it is more appropriate for us to say that in certain marginal situations they demand avowal of Jahweh, and this avowal consists precisely in abstaining from doing certain things displeasing to him.[6]

Von Rad adds that at least ancient Israel, before ossification set in, understood what the Commandments meant.

> Israel regarded the will of Jahweh as extremely flexible, ever and again adapting itself to each situation where there had been religious, political, or economic change. . . . Jahweh's will for justice positively never stood absolutely above time for Israel, for every generation was summoned anew to hearken to it as valid for itself and to make it out for itself. This once again makes clear that the commandments were not a law, but an event, with which Jahweh specifically confronted every generation in its own *hic et nunc,* and to which it had to take up its position.[7]

What was said on Sinai in effect was that "there are moral implications of accepting Yahweh's love, and these

[5] Ibid., p. 194.
[6] Ibid., p. 195.
[7] Ibid., p. 199.

negative commandments I give you specify some of the things that simply will not appear in the lives of those who love me. But how you respond positively to my love is something you yourself will know in different times and places if you really believe in me and my love."

The distinguishing characteristic of the followers of Yahweh is not so much that there are certain kinds of things they do not do as that they believe in his love and respond to it. Their response will have a profound effect on their behavior, but Yahweh is not attempting to describe that behavior in any detailed, legal code. That in later times Israel attempted to create a moral and legal system and identify it with the response to Yahweh's love only serves to measure how poorly that nation understood what transpired on Sinai. However, those ancient Israelites who gathered at the festival at Shechem realized that what happened on Sinai was only in a very minor sense concerned with morality and ethics. It was a reenactment of an experience of encounter with a powerful, passionate, and loving God.

There will continue to be, no doubt, vigorous resistance to the idea that Israel and Christianity are not basically ethical systems at all. Every religious symbol system has an ethical counterpart. As Clifford Geertz has observed, "Ethos is the reverse side of the coin of mythos." A myth tells you what is the nature of the Real and also inevitably implies how man behaves in response to the Real. The Sinai covenant symbol of a God who pushes himself into human events with a passionate love obviously prescribes an ethic by which men love one another. The way this love can or should be exercised is left largely to man's own freely determined, love-motivated decisions in time and place. Certain broad guidelines are set down. That is all Yahweh is going to do. Neither the religion of Sinai nor its offspring, the religion of Easter, contains anything in its basic symbol system which authorizes the elaboration of detailed, legalistic ethical codes, which can lay claim to specify the requirements of the Jewish or the Christian life. Yahweh wants faith and love. He has no need for legalistic codes.[8]

A friend of mine suggested that instead of a book about the Ten Commandments, it might be more appropriate to write one about the New Sins. (Ronald Knox once wrote a hilarious essay on the subject.)

It may be necessary for the Roman Catholic Church to have a code of canon law with more than two thousand rules (though that issue may be debatable), but it should be clear that the code of canon law is a set of bylaws of a particular time-space development of an institutional structure. Such a code has nothing to do with being a Christian and responding to God's love. Indeed, one could keep every single one of the canons (some are rather difficult to violate) and still not be a Christian at all. We modern men think we are categorically different from our predecessors. Everything we do has little continuity with the past, so obviously there have to be new sins, sins that only sophisticated, secular men who have "come of age" can commit. I would suggest that a development of a list of new sins would be simply one more exercise in legalism. For the Israelite and the Christian there is but one sin: not to love the Lord our God with our whole heart, our whole mind, and our whole soul. All other sins are merely the result of that basic infidelity. Refusing to respond to Yahweh's love is nothing new in

---

[8] I abstain in this book from commenting on the elaborate requirements of Jewish law. Like the code of canon law, these can be justified, I suppose, by particular circumstances of time and space. I presume that no devout Jew, however, would equate the precise fulfillment of the law with the obligation to "love the Lord your God with your whole heart and your whole mind and your whole soul." In any case, a Catholic writer has more than enough to do to cope with the legalisms of his own religious community without offering unsolicited and uninformed advice to others.

the human condition. As Exodus tells us somewhat rue-
fully, even in the desert around Sinai, there were many
gods to worship, indeed, to whore with. If good old Yahweh expected people to remain faithful for very long, the
book of Exodus seems to say, he was disabused of that
idea in short order.

Yahwistic religion, then, doesn't ask much from us in
the way of detailed behavior. On the contrary, it asks
merely one thing; but if we give Yahweh that one thing,
we have given him everything. For if we really believe
in his passionate *hesed*, then our whole lives will be
transformed.

It is much easier to elaborate lengthy, detailed ethical
and legal requirements than to turn ourselves over to
Yahweh's *hesed*. The advantage of a legal code is that it
can be fulfilled. It may require a great effort, tremendous
sacrifice, vast amounts of pain and suffering, but at some
point we will have kept all the requirements and honored
all the rules and then we can sit back and relax and say,
"See, Yahweh. We have done just what we were supposed
to and now we are your true followers."

Yahweh will say, "Not yet." He will explain that holiness does not come from making and keeping rules. Whatever holiness we have comes from the fact that a God
who loves us has chosen us for his people and we are by
definition holy. We do not become holy through effort;
we rather accept the holiness that Yahweh has tendered
us. The trouble with Yahweh's gifts is that there are
strings attached; once we have accepted them, we realize
that what he wants from us is not specific legal and ritual
behavior but our total lives, our complete response with
enthusiastic trust, confidence, and love. There is no limit
to the demands of Yahweh's love. He is not about to let
us sit back and say we have done everything we had to.
Like any passionate lover, Yahweh refuses to be content
with the ritualization of a relationship. He will not accept

from us what so many husbands and wives accept from each other—a "settling down" of a marriage relationship in which everything has become routine with no excitement or adventure. Yahweh wants a romance that never ends. He will be content with nothing less. That is the reason why the stipulations he sets down in his covenant are broad and general and deal only with the outermost limits of human morality. The Sinai covenant does not deny that ethical and moral systems are important for human life; it simply asserts that in the final analysis these systems have little to do with Yahwistic religion.

So, lists of sins, new or old, may well be useful and appropriate as guidelines to assist men in the difficult ethical judgments they must make in their lives. The follower of Yahweh is different in his approach to these ethical problems not because he has a different set of ethical principles but because his personality and his being is pervaded with a faith in God's love and a trusting confidence in his response to the fundamental graciousness of Reality. He does his best to make the proper ethical decisions according to the wisdom of ethical systems, but he makes them from the perspective of one who has been on Sinai and knows that Yahweh loves him. However, he understands that his moral decisions, while they may be influenced by his faith in God's love and are in their shape and style a consequence of that love, are not to be confused with the love of Yahweh, much less to be thought of as a means of earning that love. Yahweh once complained to Israel that he was appalled by the stench of their sacrifices. I should think he would be equally appalled by the stench of our ongoing efforts to convert the revelation of his love into a rigid moral code.

It is now possible to understand the importance of a rather strange event described in Chapter 19 of Exodus. God calls Moses to Sinai; he points out that he brought Israel out of Egypt as on eagle's wings; he informs him that they are a treasured possession among all the peoples, a kingdom of priests and a holy nation. Then the Lord informs Moses that he will come in a thick cloud and the people will hear his voice. Moses tells the people that they must purify and discipline themselves in preparation for the holy event that is to occur. Finally, after three days of waiting, there is thunder and lightning and clouds; the mountain trembles and there is fire and a blaring horn. The people are warned not to draw close to the mountain. It is a marvelous and awful event; great things are afoot: The Lord is about to utter his covenant!

One can well imagine that the participants of the Shechem festival thrilled at the retelling of the story. The drama of the imagery must have stirred their hearts and made their blood beat faster. A great religious event was about to occur once again.

The nineteenth chapter of Exodus makes it as clear as possible to us that we are dealing with a mighty and profound religious experience. If after all the thunder and lightning, the trembling of the earth, and the sound of the horn, the best Yahweh was able to do was to tell people not to commit adultery, bear false witness, kill, and steal, then he would have produced one of the great anticlimaxes in all history. What was revealed in the twentieth chapter of Exodus was the revelation of God's loving care for his people, a *hesed*. God made a covenant, a *berith*, and the world was changed.

Chapter 19, then, tells us what is happening. It is both an anticipation of and a commentary on Chapter 20. It makes clear for anybody who has eyes to read that the principal event in Chapter 20 is a revelation of a commitment of Yahweh to his people. Anything else that occurs there can only be understood as part of that commitment. It is simply impossible in the light of the anticipation and commentary contained in Chapter 19 to view Chapter 20 or any part of it as being fundamentally the establishment of an ethical system or a moral law. God revealed not the law but himself.

Before we turn to the actual content of that revelation there are two problems that must be noted. First, relatively little has been said thus far about the "monotheism" of Hebrew religion, mostly because it appears now that monotheism is less an important part of the Israelite religion than we once had thought. In the early years, there was no explicit denial of the existence of other gods besides Yahweh. Israel was to stay away from those "strange gods," who were obviously inferior to Yahweh, and Israel's principal concern was to be the existence of Yahweh, not the non-existence of other gods. The important thing in the Sinai revelation was not the proclamation of one god, but rather the proclamation of the kind of God the God of Israel really was. In later years, the Israelites would deduce that if Yahweh is that kind of God, the other gods or "powers" are of trivial importance and cannot be said to exist in the same way Yahweh exists. Was Moses a monotheist? In some sense, of course, he was, but the important thing is not whether or not he was a monotheist, but what kind of monotheist he was. William Foxwell Albright answers the question:

> If by "monotheist" is meant a thinker with views specifically like those of Philo Judaeus or Rabbi Aquiba, of St. Paul or St. Augustine, of Mohammed or Maimonides, of St. Thomas or Calvin, of Mordecai Kaplan or H. N. Wieman, Moses was not one. If, on the other hand, the term "monotheist" means one who teaches the existence of only one God, the creator of everything, the source of justice, who is equally powerful in Egypt, in the desert, and in Palestine, who has no sexuality and no mythology, who is human in form but cannot be seen by human

eye and cannot be represented in any form—then
the founder of Yahwism was certainly a monotheist.[9]

The important thing about Yahweh, then, is not that he
was the only God but rather that he was a God who
made a covenant with his people.

The other question is whether Israel's God is anthropomorphic. Many moderns are deeply offended by the
attribution of human characteristics to gods. They are
willing to believe in God, perhaps, but certainly not in a
"personal" God. Some social researchers delight in point-
ing out the decline in our belief in a personal God.
(Researchers always seem to assume, incidentally, that
there was once a time of greater belief in a personal God
than there is now.) The trouble with the use of the word
"personal" as an adjective modifying the word "God" is
that the meaning is not at all clear. For many of us, perhaps most of us, "personal" means "human." No one, not
even the wildest Israelite anthropomorphist, believed God
was human in the sense we are human. The issue is not
whether God is "like us" but whether the Ultimate Reality
is capable of entering into a love relationship with those
of us who are less than Ultimate.

There is a certain kind of pseudo-sophisticated agnosticism that is willing to concede some sort of divine
principle yet denies that that "divine principle" could
possibly be concerned with us. This position obviously
goes back before Sinai and turns God either into the in-
different Kronos or high god or into some mountain cousin
of El Shaddai, who loses track of his people when they
get too far away from his own mountain. If one is willing
to postulate some fundamental principle in the universe,
it escapes me why that fundamental principle is to be de-
nied the capacity for love. I suppose that it is a great
leap of faith to admit that there is a Real. I should think

[9] Albright, *From the Stone Age to Christianity*, op. cit., p. 207.

it would be a relatively less important leap to concede that the Real is capable of love.

My problem is trying to figure out how anything can exist. By rights, it seems to me, there should be nothing. Once something is, especially such a creature as man, capable of knowledge and love, then I see no great intellectual problem in accepting the notion that love is at the core of Reality. How come man? Once there is man, then God is rather less of a problem. But that is an intellectual and philosophical statement of the issue. The profound difficulty with a God who loves is not intellectual at all but religious. One can readily concede the plausibility of his existence and still be offended and frightened by the necessity of responding to him.

Bishop Robinson in his *Honest to God* (misunderstanding Paul Tillich, I think) takes serious offense at anthropomorphic notions of God. I fail to understand how a man can cope with God in any other than human terms. If we are to speak of him at all, we must speak of him with human words. (And presumably we can dismiss as religiously irrelevant those logicians who wish to refuse us permission to speak of God. The human race will simply not take such prohibition seriously.) When man postulates that God is Thou, he does so because there is no other way to speak of him. He understands that God is a Thou in a different way than his human friends are thou, yet he is asserting his conviction that God loves. How can anything that is Thou not love?

My friend Gregory Baum, in his extraordinarily insightful and helpful book *Man Becoming*, suggests that thinking of and speaking to God as a Thou is not appropriate because it imprisons God in our own conceptions. I do not see how else one can be faithful to the Jewish and Christian traditions of a loving God unless one thinks of him, analogously at least, as a Thou. If Father Baum can produce a set of categories and sym-

bols by which we can think of ourselves as dealing with
a loving Reality which need not be called Thou, I will
happily accept them. Until such symbols are produced,
then I am afraid that most of us have no other choice
than to conceptualize, however inadequately, the ultimate
loving Reality as a Thou.

One theologian put it to me this way: "It would not
be appropriate to deny to the deity perfection of those
human characteristics that we speak of as knowledge and
love." I suppose that this is a precise and legitimate
theological way of putting it, though as poetry and symbol, the theologian's words are worthless; but once he is
prepared to concede that it would be improper to deny
to God the perfections of those things in man that we
call knowledge and love, the theologian is really no different than the ancient Israelite arguing with Yahweh.
The latter's sense of poetry and imagery may be far more
exuberant, but it does not follow that the former really
knows anything more about God.

It would be arrogant of us to assume that the simple
anthropomorphisms of the ancient Israelite tribesman
were either naïve or ignorant. He was no more unaware,
I daresay, than is the modern theologian that we can only
speak analogously of God. The cultural context in which
he found himself made it less necessary, perhaps, than
today constantly to remind all present that the vocabulary was analogous. On the other hand, neither was he
quite as likely as some modern theologians to get so hung
up on the use of words as to become incapable of saying
anything about God.

I am certainly not denying that there are dangers in
anthropomorphic categories. They have led to abuses in
the past and they will probably lead to more in the
future; but because some people misunderstand poetry
and insist on taking it literally, it does not follow that

poetry should be abolished or that we should conclude that poetic imagery tells us nothing about Reality.

William Foxwell Albright has some appropriate comments to make on this subject, too:

> . . . it cannot be emphasized too strongly that the anthropomorphic conception of Yahweh was absolutely necessary if the God of Israel was to remain a God of the individual Israelite as well as of the people as a whole. For the limited few who are natural mystics or have learned to employ certain methods to attain ecstatic state, the theological concepts attached to deity matter relatively little; there is a striking parallelism between the psychology of mysticism in Judaism, Islam, Buddhism, and Christianity. For the average worshipper, however, it is very essential that his god be a divinity who can sympathize with his human feelings and emotions, a being whom he can love and fear alternately, and to whom he can transfer the holiest emotions connected with memories of father and mother and friend. In other words, it was precisely the anthropomorphism of Yahweh which was essential to the initial success of Israel's religion. Like man at his noblest the God of Israel might be in form and affective reactions, but there was in Him none of the human frailties that make the Olympian deities of Greece such charming poetic figures and such unedifying examples. All the human characteristics of Israel's deity were exalted; they were projected against a cosmic screen and they served to interpret the cosmic process as the expression of God's creative word and eternally active will.[10]

Since I am committed to the notion that symbols and poetry are not merely effective means of describing Reality but are in fact the only effective means of describing the

[10] Albright, op. cit., p. 202.

Ultimate Reality, I shall not hesitate to use anthropomor-phic terminology throughout this book. I would remind all nit-picking theologians that I am well aware that I am using my language analogously.

But I am further aware that no matter what one's language, the fundamental theme of the Sinaitic revela-tion is that God is a loving God. The trouble with our anthropomorphic imagery is not that it leads us to be-lieve in a love that is not there, but rather that no matter how brilliant or daring it may be, it is much less than adequate as a description of the length and breadth, the height and the depth of Yahweh's love for his people.

CHAPTER 5

I AND THOU

"I am Yahweh your God who brought you out of the land of Egypt, the house of bondage. You shall have no other gods beside me."

Verses 2 and 3 of Chapter 20 of the book of Exodus are the preamble and the historical prelude characteristic of the covenant form. Yahweh identifies himself and he describes his vast relationship with his people. Both the identification and description are starkly simple, bald statements of fact. So simple are they that we may miss the point that they contain the core of both the Jewish and the Christian religious traditions. Indeed, the whole of Yahwism is summed up in the first phrase, "I am Yahweh your God." It affirms that there is an I-Thou relationship between God and his people, a relationship of personal intimacy in which the people belong to Yahweh, but Yahweh also belongs to the people. This is the whole story of both Judaism and Christianity. All else is commentary and explication.

How many times as children did we recite the Ten Commandments, mindlessly repeating the sentence "I am the Lord thy God; thou shalt not have strange gods before me." It was an easy commandment to remember because it had a certain rhythm to it, and we could confidently begin our recitation because we knew we wouldn't stumble over the first component of the Decalogue. We didn't know exactly what it meant, of course. We were told that we shouldn't build idols, an explanation which didn't quite make sense considering all the statues in our churches. No one taught us that it was the central expression of our faith—mostly, I suppose, because none of our teachers knew it was the central statement of our faith. Nor did it seem to occur to anybody why God could possibly care whether we took strange gods seriously. Why should he be offended if we went to an occasional fortuneteller or had someone read our tea leaves?

As we shall see in more detail in the next chapter, we are not to seek after other gods precisely because such idolatry violates the intimate love of the covenant relationship. Yahweh has pledged himself to be our God and that relationship of intimate love is violated if we have other gods instead of him. The "command" part of the first commandment flows from the nature of an intimate relationship, and the important part of these verses of Exodus is not the command but the description of the relationship from which the command flows.

Professor J. G. Williams beautifully describes what Yahweh's commitment in verse 2 means:

> It means that the Power which governs the planets in their courses, causes water to evaporate, the vegetation to blossom, makes the human heart beat and the human mind think is a power who can and does identify himself with the word "I." This "I" does not simply stand over against us; this "I" surrounds us, envelops us, constitutes us. This is the "I" which cannot help but disturb, indeed overwhelm us if it is heard at all.[1]

[1] J. G. Williams, *Ten Words of Freedom: An Introduction to the Faith of Israel.* Philadelphia: Fortress Press, 1971, p. 70.

This "I" who envelops and surrounds us and proclaims himself our God tells us his name is Yahweh. There has been endless scholarly debate about the meaning of the name. Today, there seems to be some broad agreement that it is a fragment of a longer name, Yahweh-Aser-Yi-weh, in Albright's translation, "He who brings into being whatever comes into being." Therefore, in its root meaning, the name proclaims Yahweh as the all-powerful creator. However, we should remember that the Israelites were not a metaphysical people. They certainly could not understand the idea "the essence of God is his existence." Nor were they sophisticated in etymology; they may have had only vague notions of all the implications of the name by which they called upon God. We must be content with the conclusion that the name Yahweh indicated to them that their God was a powerful God; indeed, more powerful than all the other gods—so powerful in fact that he could legitimately demand that all other inferior gods be ignored. A speculative philosophy of creation was as unlikely in the desert as was a speculative theory of monotheism. It was sufficient for the Israelites to know that Yahweh dominated *everything*. Their later adaptation of the Babylonian cosmological materials indicated how decisively superior they believed Yahweh's power was to all the other powers in the universe. Yahweh was the all-powerful creative force. If we asked the desert tribes whether he created *ex nihilo* they would not have known what we were talking about, and they wouldn't have much cared.

We do not fully appreciate the heroism in the covenant religious conception. It meant that the people who were committed to the pact with Yahweh would abandon forever dealing with the "powers" now that they belonged to The Power. They could no longer bargain with the rain gods or the fertility gods or the tribal gods. Now they must commit themselves to trusting totally the Power

on which all other powers in the universe depend, realiz-
ing that they are depending totally on the gracious love
which he has promised them. Walter Harrelson describes
Yahweh's followers:

> If God will tolerate no rivals, how can a people take
> account in their worship of the presence of the dark
> powers that threaten to destroy them? What is to
> be done with the indubitable power of evil, of malev-
> olence, of rottenness in this world? Must God be
> blamed for it all? Or must man bear all the blame if
> God is freed of responsibility? Worship clearly repre-
> sents a response to the Holy that is designed, among
> other things, to ward off the powers of chaos and
> destruction. How is one to turn the power of evil
> into power for man's good, if in principle demonic
> forces and other gods are denied existence? Israel's
> theological answer—clearly not accepted by all mem-
> bers of the community at all times—is that Yahweh
> brings evil upon his people for their faithlessness to
> his will, and the same faithlessness affects the nat-
> ural order. Worship of God, then, offers a means for
> evoking God's power to forgive, to restore, to heal a
> broken humanity and a wounded earth. And fidelity
> to God's will in daily life offers the means for the
> earth's continuing fruitfulness and for God's continu-
> ing blessings upon his people.[2]

In the desert, Israel encountered the Holy, the Totally
Other, the Reality simultaneously fascinating and ter-
rifying. All religious experiences are an encounter of some
sort with the Holy, but the Holy as perceived by Israel
was both more powerful and more benign than that encountered in any religious experience before or since.
(I here presume that the Easter experience of the apostles
is fundamentally a continuation of Sinai.) The Holy was

[2] Walter Harrelson, *From Fertility Cult to Worship*, op. cit.,
p. 13.

not passive, was not withdrawn; rather, it was creative, active, demanding, involved. It was an incredibly dynamic power, but a power that was essentially loving. The depths and the power of this holiness are, as Gerhard von Rad tells us, essentially manifested in the first commandment in "Jahweh's curt claim . . . to be the only God worshipped."[3] Von Rad continues:

> This intolerant claim to exclusive worship is something unique in the history of religion, for in antiquity the cults were on easy terms with one another and left devotees a free hand to ensure a blessing for themselves from other gods as well.[4]

Israel's choice of the covenant symbolism to convey its experience of the Holy made it inevitable that the exclusivity of worship became a central theme of Israelite religion. Note well what happens. Israel had an experience of the Holy, an experience of Reality that was almost unbearably powerful. So powerful—and so good—is this Holy perceived to be that the human response to it is to say, "There can be no other Holiness besides this Holiness." God did not create the covenant symbolism, Israel did. The covenant idea described the nature of Israel's relationship with the Holiness in terms of a demand for exclusive love. The covenant was the tool Israel chose to describe primarily for itself but also for others the nature of the Holy it encountered. Speculative monotheism and the doctrine of creation *ex nihilo* would come later, much later. Even the beautiful marriage symbolism would come somewhat later. In its rawest and most primitive form, Israel experienced Power—Power that was both overwhelming and gracious, Power demanding response. In the time and place in which Israel found itself, an exclusive I-Thou relationship, precluding any dealing with

[3] Von Rad, *Old Testament Theology*, Vol. I, op. cit., p. 207.
[4] Ibid., p. 208.

lesser gods, was the best symbolism available for describing what had happened. More than that must be said, however. For all our progress, we may not have come up today with a better symbolism of man's relationship to God than that contained in the insight that God is an "I" who wishes to relate to us as "Thou."

If we understand that the whole history of Israelite thought is an attempt to clarify the experience of the powerful but benign Yahweh, we can then begin to make some sense out of the Old Testament religious poetry, which frequently seems so peculiar to us. Thus, Yahweh continues to dominate creation:

Lift your eyes and look.
Who made these stars
if not he who drills them like an army,
calling each one by name?
So mighty is his power, so great his strength,
that not one fails to answer. (Isaiah 40:26)

I it was who made the earth,
and created man who is on it.
I it was who spread out the heavens with my hands
and now give orders to their whole array. (Isaiah 45:12)

He makes both the dawn and the darkness:

For he it was who formed the mountains, created the wind,
reveals his mind to man,
makes both dawn and dark,
and walks on the top of the heights of the world;
Yahweh, God of Sabaoth, is his name. (Amos 4:13)

It is he who made the Pleiades and Orion,
who turns the dusk to dawn
and day to darkest night.
He summons the waters of the sea
and pours them over the land.
Yahweh is his name. (Amos 5:8)

He measures the water in the hollow of his hand:

> Who was it measured the water of the sea in the hollow of
>   his hand
> and calculated the dimensions of the heavens,
> gauged the whole earth to the bushel,
> weighed the mountains in scales,
> the hills in a balance? (Isaiah 40:12)

He gives breath and spirit to those who walk the earth:

> Thus says God, Yahweh,
> he who created the heavens and spread them out,
> who gave shape to the earth and what comes from it,
> who gave breath to its people
> and life to the creatures that move in it: (Isaiah 42:5)

If Yahweh is superior to the gods of fertility, it still must not be thought that he is not involved in fertility. On the contrary, fertility is Yahweh's gift to men. It is not Baal but Yahweh who bestows the fruits of the soil:

> She would not acknowledge, not she,
> that I was the one who was giving her
> the corn, the wine, the oil,
> and who freely gave her that silver and gold
> of which they have made Baals.

> That is why, when the time comes, I mean to withdraw my
>   corn,
> and my wine, when the season for it comes.
> I will retrieve my wool, my flax,
> that were intended to cover her nakedness;
> so will I display her shame before her lovers' eyes
> and no one shall rescue her from my power.
> I will lay her vines and fig trees waste,
> those of which she used to say,
> "These are the pay my lovers gave me";

I am going to make them into thickets
for the wild beasts to ravage.
I will put an end to all her rejoicing,
her feasts, her New Moons, her sabbaths
and all her solemn festivals.
I mean to make her pay for all the days
when she burnt offerings to the Baals
and decked herself with rings and necklaces
to court her lovers,
forgetting me.
It is Yahweh, who is speaking. (Hosea 2:10–15)

He, further, is the one who is responsible for the progeny
of men and beasts and fruit of the field:

He will love you and bless you and increase your numbers;
he will bless the fruit of your body and the produce of
your soil, your corn, your wine, your oil, the issue of your
cattle, the young of your flock, in the land he swore to
your fathers he would give you. (Deuteronomy 7:13)

They will come and shout for joy on the heights of Zion,
they will throng towards the good things of Yahweh:
corn and oil and wine,
sheep and oxen;
their soul will be like a watered garden,
they will sorrow no more. (Jeremiah 31:12)

He gives and withholds rain:

He will send rain for the seed you sow in the ground,
and the bread that the ground provides will be rich
and nourishing. Your cattle will graze, that day, in
wide pastures. (Isaiah 30:23)

And it is most sure that if you faithfully obey the
commandments I enjoin on you today, loving Yahweh your
God and serving him with all your heart and all your
soul, I will give your land rain in season, autumn rain

and spring, so that you may harvest your corn, your wine,
your oil; (Deuteronomy 11:13–14)

Come, we must fear Yahweh our God
who gives the rain, the early rain
and the later, at the right time of year,
who assures us
of weeks appointed for harvest. (Jeremiah 5:24)

But while Yahweh is responsible for the blessings of
fertility, he is himself superior to the process. Yahweh
dominates fertility; he is not a fertility god.

It is no longer thought that Yahweh was originally a
storm god, though surely there were storm gods in the
Israelite religious background. Nevertheless, the Israelites
thought of the power of Yahweh when they experienced
the tremendous natural forces of storm, earthquake, and
volcanic eruption.

Then the earth quivered and quaked,
the foundations of the mountains trembled
(they quivered because he was angry);
from his nostrils a smoke ascended,
and from his mouth a fire that consumed
(live embers were kindled at it).

He bent the heavens and came down,
a dark cloud under his feet;
he mounted a cherub and flew,
and soared on the wings of the wind.

Darkness he made a veil to surround him,
his tent a watery darkness, dense cloud;
before him a flash enkindled
hail and fiery embers.

Yahweh thundered from heaven,
the Most High made his voice heard;
he let his arrows fly and scattered them,
launched the lightnings and routed them.

The bed of the seas was revealed,
the foundations of the world were laid bare,
at your muttered threat, Yahweh
at the blast of your nostrils' breath. (Psalm 18:7–15)

the earth rocked,
the heavens deluged at God's coming,
at the coming of God, the God of Israel.

God, you rained a downpour of blessings,
when your heritage was faint you gave it strength;
your family found a home, where you
in your goodness, God, provided for the needy. (Psalm 68:
8–10)

Eloah is coming from Teman,
and the Holy One from Mount Paran.
His majesty veils the heavens,
the earth is filled with his glory.

His brightness is like the day,
rays flash from his hands,
that is where his power lies hidden.

Plague goes in front of him,
fever follows on his heels.

When he stands up he makes the earth tremble,
with his glance he makes the nations quake.
Then the ancient mountains are dislodged,
the everlasting hills sink down,
his pathway from of old.

I have seen the tents of Cushan terrified,
the pavilions of the land of Midian shuddering.

Yahweh, is your anger blazing against the rivers,
or your fury against the sea,
that you come mounted on your horses,
on your victorious chariots?

You uncover your bow,
you ply its string with arrows.

You trench the soil with torrents;
the mountains shiver when they see you;
great floods sweep on their way,
the abyss roars aloud,
high it lifts its hands.

Sun and moon stay in their houses,
avoiding the flash of your arrows,
the gleam of your glittering spear.

Raging, you stride the earth,
in anger you trample the nations.

You have marched to save your people,
to save your own anointed;
you have beaten down the wicked man's house,
bared its foundations to the rock.

With your shafts you have pierced the leader of his warriors
who stormed out with shouts of joy to scatter us,
as if they meant to devour some poor wretch in their lair.

You have trampled the sea with your horses,
the surge of great waters. (Habakkuk 3:3–15)

"Yahweh, when you set out from Seir,
as you trod the land of Edom,
earth shook, the heavens quaked,
the clouds dissolved into water.
The mountains melted before Yahweh,
before Yahweh, the God of Israel. . . ." (Judges 5:4–5)

But Yahweh is not only powerful, he is also wise. Thus,
for example, in Isaiah 28:23–29, Yahweh's wisdom in
directing the natural cycles is extolled:

Listen closely to my words,
be attentive and understand what I am saying.
Does the ploughman do nothing but plough
and turn the soil and harrow it?
Will he not, after he has levelled it,

scatter fennel, sow cummin,
put in wheat and barley
and, on the edges, spelt?
He has been taught this discipline
by his God who instructs him.

For fennel must not be crushed,
nor a drag be rolled over cummin;
fennel must be beaten with a stick,
and cummin with a flail.
Does a man crush wheat? No;
he does not thresh it endlessly.
When he has rolled the drag over it
he winnows it without crushing it.
This too comes from Yahweh Sabaoth,
whose advice is always admirable,
whose deeds are very great.

And in Job 5:23, the covenant theology is applied even to Yahweh's relationship with nature:

You shall have a pact with the stones of the field,
and live in amity with wild beasts.

But from the point of view of the Israelites, far more impressive than Yahweh's manifestations of his power and wisdom in the works of nature was his self-revelation in his dealing with his people. For as the second half of verse 2, Chapter 20, of Exodus identifies him, he is Yahweh, who has brought them out of Egypt, the house of bondage. Some of the mightiest hymns of the Old Testament describe the marvels of God's intervention on behalf of his people. We used to recite them mindlessly: Psalms 77, 78, 105, and 106. They were strange, slightly pompous oriental poetry. We did not realize that we were dealing with liturgical hymns that were, if not actually part of the ceremony of covenant renewal, at least a celebration of God's covenant with his people. In Psalm 77, verses 13–20, for example, the Israelites sang of their primordial religious experience of a God who was involved with them.

> God, your ways are holy!
> What god so great as God?
> You are the God who did marvellous things
> and forced nations to acknowledge your power,
> with your own arm redeeming your people,
> the sons of Jacob and Joseph.
>
> When the waters saw it was you, God,
> when the waters saw it was you, they recoiled,
> shuddering to their depths.
> The clouds poured down water,
> the sky thundered,
> your arrows darted out.
>
> Your thunder crashed as it rolled,
> your lightning lit up the world,
> the earth shuddered and quaked.
> You strode across the sea,
> you marched across the ocean,
> but your steps could not be seen.
> You guided your people like a flock
> by the hands of Moses and Aaron.

And in Psalm 106:43–48, Israel acknowledged its weakness in responding to the demands of the covenant; but it also celebrated the fact that if Israel forgot the covenant, Yahweh did not.

> Time and again he rescued them,
> but they went on defying him deliberately
> and plunging deeper into wickedness;
> even so, he took pity on their distress
> each time he heard them calling.

For their sake, he remembered his covenant,
he relented in his great love,
making their captors mitigate
the harshness of their treatment.

Yahweh our God and saviour,
gather us from among the pagans,
to give thanks to your holy name
and to find our happiness in praising you.

Blessed be Yahweh the God of Israel,
from all eternity and for ever!
Here, all the people are to say, "Amen."

Israel's encounter with God, then, was not merely an experience of "nature mysticism." Yahweh, indeed, worked in the sun and the moon, the stars and the fertility cycles, and the storms and volcanoes and earthquakes. But he was recognized as dominating these events because Israel had encountered him in another context, a context of his being involved in their *history*. Yahweh was not first recognized in the storm-volcano theophany of Sinai; he was first encountered when he brought Israel out of Egypt.

The "Thou" who is Israel's God is a God of power and love *and* action. He is involved not merely in gracious affection in *hesed* for his people. He is also involved in the course of human events, and the eschatological and messianic expectations which Israel would later develop were but a natural and logical conclusion from its conviction that God is directing the course of human events toward a *purpose*. Israel might not have understood Father Teilhard's idea about progression toward an "omega point," but it had the same fundamental insight. Indeed, one perhaps ought to go further and say that if it had not been for the Sinai experience, Teilhard would have never thought of the "omega point." Nor, indeed, would the

human race have developed the concern about history
and evolutionary viewpoint or the secular, political eschatology which is so typical of liberal progressivism in
Europe and the United States. For it is in the notion
that Yahweh brought us out of Egypt that we have the
root origins of the belief in progress. Human affairs are
not an endless cycle, constantly repeating itself in an endless series of representations and reincarnations. Human
events do not follow routine paths, as do the cycles of
fertility and the progression of the stars across the heavens.
Because God directs the course of human affairs, there
is a beginning, a middle, and, as Israel came to understand eventually, an end—a "day" of Yahweh in which
his work is finally accomplished.

It is one of the paradoxes of the contemporary world
that men are no longer ready to believe that God *acts* in
history but are willing to believe in historical progress and
in the possibility of secular eschatology. The belief in
human progress is one of the driving forces of Western
culture, even though that belief has recently eroded somewhat under one of those periodic attacks of romantic
pessimism. The appeal and attractiveness of Charles A.
Reich's *The Greening of America* is to be found precisely
in the fact that it is a progressive, eschatological response
to pessimism. It is a reassertion of the basic Western as-
sertion that history has point and purpose.

I have always been baffled as to why men can believe
in progress and not believe in God (whatever it means
"not to believe in God"). For if there is progress in human events, if there is a development toward a goal, it
certainly cannot be attributed to Darwinian evolutionary
process, for man has evolved biologically relatively little
in the last hundreds of thousands of years. If, indeed, we
are moving in a direction there is some Force directing us,
and if one is willing to concede the existence of that
Force, it seems to me that one implicitly concedes that the

Force is benign, else why would it be directing us toward improvement and growth? This benign, directive, evolutionary Force, I should think, is not much different from Yahweh on Sinai.

It is now popular and fashionable to decry belief in the progress of the human race and to predict that we are bound for disaster; but even those who announce the new apocalypse do so in a messianic and eschatological vocabulary. They demonstrate their obvious conviction that if we change our ways (if we repent of our sins, in other words), we can be saved; disaster can be averted and progress away from our present condition may then be still possible. Even those who reject the myth of progress are still caught in its categories, its rhetoric, and, on occasion, even in the style of its religious origins.

I am not prepared to try to defend the myth of progress, at least in its more simple secularized forms. But it is difficult to understand why so many people can accept progress as one of their primary intellectual and cultural perspectives and still find it hard to acknowledge some sort of "Principle" of progress. Why are they willing to buy part of the myth and not all of it? (In truth, they seem to believe the more dubious part.)

I do not know how Yahweh acts in human history. I am not sure how God is involved in human events. This is a complicated philosophical and theological question, which I think has never been really satisfactorily answered by philosophers and theologians. Perhaps it does not admit of a satisfactory answer. I often wonder why Catholic theologians seem so little aware of the process philosophy of Alfred North Whitehead and Charles Hartshorne (and the process theology of their disciples, John Cobb and Schubert Ogden). There are a number of problems with this process philosophy and theology; both its assets and liabilities are beyond the scope of this book, but at least Whitehead and his disciples had no trouble at all dealing with the notion of a God who acts. I would think that attempts to come to philosophical and theological grips with the activity of God ought to be very high on the agenda of Christian theologians.

Israel, of course, was a notoriously unspeculative and unmetaphysical people. It would have been at a complete loss to explain how Yahweh was involved in its history. It would not have known what to make of the distinction between the natural and the supernatural. It could not have responded to our question: Do you think that Sinai was an ordinary or an extraordinary intervention of God in human affairs? It only knew that it had experienced in a unique and overwhelming way the presence of Yahweh in the events of its history. Yahweh was *there*. He was, to use a modern colloquialism, "where it's at." Israel couldn't have cared less *how* he was present.

As more rational and sophisticated men, we do care *how* Yahweh works. It is certainly legitimate and appropriate for us to attempt to arrive at some explanation. Ultimately the question is not how Yahweh acts but *whether* he acts. Or, to put the issue on a somewhat more abstract and less anthropomorphic level, is Reality truly gracious? Is it loving, benign, and involved in profound concern with us? There are all kinds of reasons for saying no—and some for saying yes. But whether we decide that the Really Real loves us with a *hesed*, a loving kindness, or not cannot be resolved by philosophical debate. *How* the Real loves us is far less important than *whether* it does. Our decision about whether it does or not is as much an act of faith for us as it was for Israel at the foot of Sinai.

The other gods are excluded from Israel's cult for the simple and obvious reason that they are not Yahweh. To have anything to do with the other gods is not only unfaithful, it is foolishness. They have neither the power nor the concern nor the love that Yahweh has. The literal translation of verse 3, Chapter 20, of Exodus is "You shall not have other gods before my face." (The Hebrew words are *al panai*.) The face is not merely the front part of a man's head; it is also his presence. God's face among men (even though no one is permitted to see his face) means that God is present among men. That man may not "see" him, that is, look upon him, is not important. God is present among them, and the presence of other lesser powers is excluded. In effect God says, "Why, when you have my presence, should you need the presence of other gods?"

In Exodus 33, there is an interesting juxtaposition of two different traditions among the Israelites about the "face" of Yahweh. In 33:20, Yahweh says, "You cannot see my face, for man cannot see me and live." On the other hand, in 33:11, we are told that "Yahweh used to speak to Moses face to face, as a man speaks with his friend." The two traditions are not necessarily inconsistent. Yahweh is thought of as being present as a friend. a friend whose presence one can almost feel physically; and he is present so overwhelmingly and powerfully (in our terminology, so infinitely) that we cannot possibly grasp him with our human powers of perception or description.

It is easy to be affronted by the Sinai myth. I suspect that one of the reasons why we convert the twentieth chapter of the book of Exodus into an ethical code is that an ethical code is not so much an "insult to our intelligence" as is a God who claims to be so powerfully and lovingly involved in human events. We know that the human race needs ethical codes; we are not at all sure that it needs that sort of God; and, more importantly, we are not sure that we can believe in or accept that sort of God. Much of the history of Judaism and Christianity has consisted of attempts to fuzz the issue, to dodge the challenge of Exodus 20:2–3, to try to persuade ourselves that the important thing is to keep certain rules and not to accept entirely the incredible notion of a God who makes covenant with humans. Some moderns will tell us that in a scientific age it is difficult if not impossible to accept such a covenanting God. No one with any powers of observation would deny it, but that it is any more difficult now than in any previous age seems problematic. On the basis of the evidence available to us, most of the men who have lived since the thirteenth century B.C. who were exposed to the Sinai myth and later to the Jesus myth have done their best to avoid making a decision for or against the myths. Legalism, triumphalism, political messianism played a role in ages past functionally equivalent to that of academic, bourgeois agnosticism in the present.

It is certainly not my purpose here to attempt to persuade the reader of the validity of the Sinai myth. I merely wish to describe it, to describe what it really is as well as I can. I am not affronted if the reader rejects the myth as having no value for his religious life. I am affronted if he rejects it without knowing what it really is. Many of those who call themselves believers and many of those who call themselves unbelievers have this important thing in common: what they believe in or what they don't believe in has nothing to do with the critical myth of Sinai (and Jesus, too, for that matter). The believer believes in an essentially legalistic, organized religion; the unbeliever rejects such a religion—and also a God who is some great hangman in the sky. Neither addresses himself to the question of whether the Ultimate, the Real, the Absolute is also profound, passionate Love, a Love that is *involved* with us. That is the issue, and it has been the issue since Israel encountered Yahweh in the desert. For those who have heard of Israel's encounter, there is no other religious question that has any pertinence at all compared to the one that asks, do you believe that Reality corresponds to Israel's powerful, gracious, committed Yahweh?

There is a second question, of course: If you do, why don't you live in such a way that your faith is manifested? Perhaps the second question is more revealing than the first.

Dean M. Kelley, a Protestant administrator and scholar, has recently written about the apparent continued success of the "conservative" denominations in the United States while the more "progressive" denominations seem to have much less vitality, and, indeed, seem to be losing both commitment and membership. Kelley concludes that the conservative churches are more successful because they still provide "meaning," that is to say, they offer an interpretive system which gives their members symbols with which they can respond to the fundamental questions of human life. The progressive churches, on the other hand, are much less certain about meaning, are not at all sure what they believe in, and hence do not provide their congregations with pertinent symbol systems.

In some of Kelley's analysis it would seem that he almost blames the congregations of these churches for the fact that they have nothing in which they clearly believe. Of course, the problem is much more acute for the clergy and the organizational leadership of the churches. Many of the clerics in the more established, progressive denominations have no clear idea of what it is they believe; hence, there is a strong temptation for them to replace religious symbols with social service, political action, or quasi-professional psychotherapy. There are others in society who are specialists in social welfare, political action, and therapy; there is no reason why a congregation should take a clergyman seriously on these matters unless he demonstrates that he is both well informed and well trained. On the contrary, when a cleric indicates that his enthusiasm and moral commitment is a substitute for information and competence, his people are likely to dismiss him as not worth listening to. A persuasive case can be made, I think, for the argument that a religious leader who does have a meaningful religious symbol system to preach to his people will be taken much more seriously when he turns to social and political problems than one for whom social and political symbolism have substituted for religions symbols.

While Kelley's analysis is admirable, I do not think that there is an intrinsic reason why the more conservative churches should have a monopoly on vital religious symbols. The decline of effective religious symbols among the progressive churches is a historical accident—an accident of history which is probably beginning to happen in Roman Catholicism too. The clergy of the upper-middle-class mainline denominations are generally trained in divinity schools that are adjuncts to the secular universities. Hence, they are likely to be permeated with the paralyzing agnosticism which is for all practical purposes the official faith of most secular universities. Furthermore, since the divinity schools are on the margins of the university, the form of agnosticism which develops there is likely to be naïve and simplistic. Caught up as he is in the philosophical and methodological problems of the university environment and in the constant change of liberal academic fads, the divinity student (and usually his teacher, too) permits himself to be persuaded that God is dead, that religion is irrelevant because man has become secularized, that the religious symbols have become "broken," and that what is needed in the world is not faith but social reform. Thus social and political symbols become all-important, and religious symbols, to the extent that they are understood or accepted at all, recede into the background.

A denomination which is staffed by large numbers of such confused and troubled clerics will cease to be a religious organization in any meaningful sense of the word.

I am surely not asserting that all or even a majority of Protestant clergy think that religious symbols are not important any more (or, to use that ugly, terrible word, "relevant"). Nor am I suggesting that all or even a majority of the younger Catholic clergy have dismissed the relevance of religious symbols. I am saying that there is a strong strain in the divinity school environment toward reducing the importance of religious symbols and replacing them with other symbols. This is a historical accident, a development from the peculiar social and cultural forces of our time and one which over the long run will pass away, I suspect. In the process, however, many of the more "liberal" denominations may find themselves slowly going out of business.

I do not suggest that the social or philosophical issues of our culture ought to be ignored; but philosophical argumentation can neither establish nor disestablish the validity of religious symbols. Philosophy, in other words, can neither command nor prohibit faith. Furthermore, while social and political commitment is essential for those who accept the Sinaitic or Christian symbol systems, they are essential as a consequence, not as a substitute for them. The question a divinity school student (and quite possibly a faculty member, too) ought to ask himself is, "Do I really believe in a gracious, loving Reality?" If he does, fine. He ought to preach it. If not, perhaps he ought to find another occupation.

I address myself to the divinity school syndrome because I think that it represents in an exaggerated way the misplaced religious issue of our time (though past ages have managed to misplace it, too). Many people will say, "I'm not sure what I believe any more." As a description of an existential situation, this may be a painful though accurate statement. Indeed, no one can be

sure of what he believes in the same way one can be sure
of a mathematical theorem. Faith generates a certainty
but not that kind of certainty. However, as a persistent
religious posture, the "I'm not sure what I believe in any
more" stance is infantile; it is an attempt to escape from
making a commitment either to or against faith. When
his refusal is accompanied by a disinclination to investigate the religious sources or a scapegoating of institutional religion, then one is forced to conclude that such
a person is both psychologically and religiously imma-
ture. Organized churches make splendid scapegoats, of
course; but the validity of religious symbols have nothing
to do with the fragile human organizations that proclaim
them. Anyone who announces that he is not sure whether
he accepts the religious symbols out of his own past heritage without bothering to find out what these symbols
really say about the meaning and purpose of human life
is behaving childishly.

The pertinent question to ask someone who takes the
stance I have described is, "Do you believe in an ultimately loving and gracious Reality or don't you?" At
some point he must decide one way or the other. The
frequent response from such a person is to bring up the
problem of the existence of evil.

It is a problem well worth discussing. No satisfactory
solution of it has ever been achieved and is not likely to
be. If the problem of evil could be resolved, faith would
not be faith but merely the acceptance of something
that was logically obvious. The leap of faith cannot depend on the problem of evil being eliminated. One believes despite evil. If one believes that evil will ultimately
triumph and that Reality is not gracious and loving, then
the appropriate answer to the religious question is that
life is arbitrary, capricious, tragic, and absurd. That is at
least a stance that does not attempt to avoid the issue by
arguing about the nature of manna in the desert or was

Yahweh's voice really heard on Sinai or why isn't the church more vigorous in condemning war. I cannot argue with someone who takes such a stance. I believe he is wrong, but he has made his act of faith and I have made mine. I believe in the loving, gracious, pushy Yahweh, who told the Israelites in the desert and everyone after them that he is that God. The man who postulates an absurd and ungracious universe, or even a "random" one, does not believe it. We may respect each other as human beings, but we have very different visions of reality.

But at least he is honest and consistent, and those who refuse to face the challenge of the religious symbols, who half-believe them and half-reject them, who interpret them in such a way that they are interpreted away, are to be counted among the lukewarm of whom Jesus spoke. They are the sort of persons who stand at the foot of Sinai and ask Moses when he has come down from the mountain, "Moses, old chap, how about going back up there to work out some sort of compromise with Yahweh so that we can believe him up to a point?" Moses was, if the traditions are accurate, a very hot-tempered fellow, and I think it was probably not too safe to propose such a deal to him, and it is most unlikely that he would have ventured back up the mountain. I think if he had, all might have heard the thunder again—not of anger but of Yahweh's laughing in our faces.

CHAPTER 6

NO IDOLATRY

⁴You shall not make for yourself a sculptured image, or any likeness of what is in the heavens above, or on the earth below, or in the waters under the earth. ⁵You shall not bow down to them or serve them. For I the LORD your God am an impassioned God, visiting the guilt of the fathers upon the children, upon the third and upon the fourth generations of those who reject Me, ⁶but showing kindness to the thousandth generation of those who love Me and keep My commandments. (Exodus 20:4-6)

Most exegetes agree that the words contained in verse 4 are more ancient, and that verses 5 and 6 are a reflection from the point of view of covenant theology. It is also generally supposed that the original prohibition was against an image of Yahweh; only later was this prohibition extended to include images of other gods. In the previous verses, Yahweh had disposed of the other gods; Israel was simply not to have them. This verse is seen now as it was seen originally as God's concern with forbidding Israel to make images of him.

It would be a mistake to think that the ancient peoples identified their god with the god's image. The Old Testament railing against pagan images as though the gods themselves is perhaps something of a rhetorical exaggeration. But while the gods were distinct from their images, they were not independent of them. In Martin Noth's words:

> The basis for it [images] rather lies in the idea, widespread in the ancient world, that an image had a firm connection with the being it portrayed, and that with the help of an image a man might gain power over the being represented in the image. Israel is forbidden any image so that the people cannot even make the attempt to gain power over God or that which is of God.[1]

Yahweh had entered a covenant relationship with Israel on his own initiative. It was a free choice on his part and a free response on the part of Israel. They were to continue to relate to one another as free partners. There would be no magic, no attempt to constrain Yahweh to act in ways his human colleagues deemed appropriate. The only constraints on Yahweh were his own generosity and love. The power of Yahweh is such that it cannot be limited by images or even contained in the whole physical universe. In the fourth chapter of the book of Deuteronomy, verses 16–19, this precept of the Decalogue is repeated with more theological explanation:

> not to act wickedly and make for yourself a sculptured image in any likeness whatever, having the form of a man or a woman, the form of any beast on earth, the form of any winged bird that flies in the sky, the form of anything that creeps on the ground, the form of any fish that is in the waters below the earth. And when you look up to the sky and behold the sun and the moon and the stars, the

[1] Martin Noth, *Exodus. A Commentary.* Translated by J. S. Bowden. Philadelphia: Westminster Press, 1962, pp. 162–63.

whole heavenly host, you must not be lured into
bowing down to them or serving them. These the
LORD your God allotted to the other peoples every-
where under heaven; . . . (Deuteronomy 4:16–19)

Neither in the heavens nor in the sun, the moon, the
stars, nor anywhere in creation is there anything that can
contain Yahweh. He is holy, mysterious, beyond man's
control. He operates in human events, indeed, but on his
own initiative. He is close to them, but it is a closeness of
mystery and love. Israel's trust and confidence is based
on the bare word of God as spoken in his covenant commitment. As von Rad observes:

> Nature was not a mode of Jahweh's being; he stood
> over against it as its Creator. This then means that
> the commandment forbidding images is bound up
> with the hidden way in which Jahweh's revelation
> came about in cult and history. It would be a mis-
> take to think of the commandment simply as an
> isolated cultic peculiarity of Israel. The Jahweh whom
> Israel was so strictly forbidden to worship by means
> of an image was still the same Jahweh by whose
> hidden action in history she was continually kept in
> suspense.[2]

We must understand that in the ancient world, divine
power was thought of as lurking just behind the veil of
the physical universe. Images and idols were the pas-
sageways through the veil to the inner reality of divine
power. What Yahweh told Israel, however, was that
even though he was involved in human events—indeed,
as we shall see, deeply and passionately involved—he was
totally separated from the physical world, above not
only its external veils but also its internal "powers." It

[2] Von Rad, *Old Testament Theology*, Vol. I, op. cit., p. 218.

may have been possible, perhaps, to "break through" to other gods by way of their images, but it was impossible to break through that way to Yahweh because Yahweh wasn't there. He revealed himself not so much through the powers of the natural cycles; he directly intervened in the affairs of his people. In the covenant, he "broke through" to them, not they to him.

There may have been physical phenomena like earthquakes, volcanoes erupting, or thunderstorms related to some of Israel's desert experience of Yahweh. But their fundamental religious encounter with him had nothing to do with natural phenomena at all. They became conscious in the desert that he had made them a people; and he had done this not because they had idols of him or not because there was a storm or an earthquake. He did it because he had chosen to involve himself in their events. Yahweh was a God of history because in historical events and not in natural phenomena or in cultic worship, Israel first realized its full power.

This kind of God was completely different from any other god available to the peoples surrounding Israel. It was small wonder, then, that in times of trouble or confusion, Israel was tempted to turn to gods with whom they could deal in the old fashion. At various times, perhaps, there may have been idols even of Yahweh. The prophetic denunciation of idols in later years can only be understood as an insistence of the unique nature of Israel's original experience of Yahweh.

> The relentless shattering of cherished concepts of God which occupied the pre-exilic prophets stands in a theological relationship which is perhaps hidden, but which is, in actual fact, very close to the commandment forbidding images. Any interpretation which deals in isolation with the impossibility of representing Jahweh by an image, and which does

not see the commandment as bound up with the
totality of Jahweh's revelation, misses the crucial
point. . . .[3]

So, the prohibition of images is not merely a fussy regu-
lation that a touchy God imposes on his people to keep
them in line. It is rather an inevitable and logical consequence of the nature of the divinity that Israel encountered at Sinai.

In days gone by we generally skipped over the commandment forbidding graven images with a fairly light
heart. If we were Catholics, we had to admit that there
were statues in our churches, but we explained blithely
that while the pagans at the time of Israel believed their
gods resided in the statues, we knew better. Our statues
were only representations to remind us of God or the
saints to whom we were devoted. I am certainly not an
iconoclast of the sort of the notorious Leo the Isaurian,
who went about smashing statues in Constantinople back
in the eighth century. It is possible to have sacred images
and not vest them with sacred power. I suppose that
large numbers of Catholics did have the proper understanding of sacred images and did not in fact think that
the image gave them some kind of "stranglehold" over
the saint with whom they were dealing. I also believe
that there is psychological wisdom in the cult of the
saints. It is not inevitable that a saint be converted to a
surrogate God, who will play a role vis-à-vis us like the
one the idols played for the neighbors of Israel.

While idolatry may not have been completely absent
from the cult of the veneration of statues or the cult of
the saint in pre-conciliar Catholicism (in post-conciliar,
too, for that matter), there is a wide range of appropriate
behavior in our relationships with God. Our behavior be-

[3] Ibid., p. 218.

comes inappropriate only when it becomes magical; that is to say, when we allow ourselves to be persuaded that we have some sure-fire technique or formula for dealing with God or when we believe that we have found a method for guaranteeing that Yahweh's ways become our ways.

The problem, then, is not so much veneration of images or the cultivation of the cult of saints. The problem is idolatry in a much more fundamental sense of the word. The late Paul Tillich did us all a great service when he pointed out this more basic idolatry and defined it as "making absolute the relative."

The relative becomes absolute when anything religious—a symbol, a cult, an image, a philosophical or theological system, an ideology, an organization, a legal structure, a distribution of decision-making power—becomes more important in the practical order than the God these things are supposed to manifest. When the most important reality in my concrete, everyday religious life becomes a statue or a saint, a parish or a church organization, my own position in the ecclesiastical power structure, or Thomism or opposition to abortion or even a crusade for peace and racial justice, then I have become an idolater. I have taken something that is relative and made it absolute. I have decided that I could "break through" to Yahweh by my virtue or my zeal or my ecclesiastical importance or my commitment to the cause of his Church. Yahweh doesn't require commitment to his Church; he wants us to be committed to *him*. The Church, philosophy, theology, ideology, Catholic education, the preservation of parishes, or whatever else might involve our religious interests are only relatively important. We can fool ourselves if we believe that in these relative things we can confidently and at all times encounter Yahweh. Yahweh, on the contrary, is where he wants to be, not where we want him to be.

Tillich, particularly in his earlier years, vigorously insisted that Roman Catholicism was guilty of idolatry
because it identified divine power with ecclesiastical
structure. While he may have overdone it, I am inclined
to think that Tillich made a very important point. Surely,
on the theoretical level few Catholics would have made
such an identification, but for all practical purposes many
of us believed and many of our leaders claimed implicitly
if not explicitly that the organized Roman Church "possessed" God, and that he could only really be found in
the Church. Furthermore, we also came very close to
claiming that loyalty to the institutional Church was the
same thing as religion and was the appropriate worship
of God. The triumphalism so dearly beloved by the Roman curia for several centuries has by no means been
driven from the field even today. It was idolatry pure and
simple. I would also insist that the identification (in deeds
if not in words) by many bishops of the cause of God with
the preservation of their own ecclesiastical power is also
idolatry. The late John Courtney Murray used to say of a
prominent archbishop (and who that archbishop was
varied from circumstance to circumstance), "He is an absolutely honest man. He would never tell a lie save for
the good of the Church." Murray was joking, but not
really; and it is a commonplace that many American bishops have lied so often to their priests and their people
that no one believes them any more.* They will justify
their deception on the grounds that it was necessary "for
the good of the Church," though they may not use those
words exactly. But, of course, this is to make the "good of
the Church" absolute. What is important is the survival
of the Church as an ecclesiastical institution and not as
a proclamation of the Good News of honesty, integrity,

* Please observe that I said "many"—not most, not a majority,
but "many."

and trust, which, one would have thought, is the purpose
of the Church's existence.

It does seem astonishing that these men apparently do
not understand that if the Church is worth preserving
and if it is to be preserved, then God will preserve
it, not the hierarchy. Whenever we come to believe that
the accomplishment of a religious goal depends uniquely
and solely on us, we have become idolaters. And worse
than that, we do not really believe that Yahweh is our
God and that he has made a covenant with us, a covenant
that he will promote with loving-kindness.

I am not advocating administrative irresponsibility. I
am insisting that the exercise of the administrative responsibility is a relative good and not an absolute one. We do
the best we can, and if it be God's will that our work suc-
ceeds, then we rejoice. If it does not succeed, then we
must still be convinced that in the long run Yahweh will
triumph. If we don't believe this, we don't believe in Yahweh and we have no business in a position of ecclesiastical
responsibility.

It is easy, of course, to criticize bishops. After all, they
do so many things worth criticizing. But the temptation
to idolatry is by no means limited to the hierarchy. It
takes great courage to yield our own convictions, de-
sires, aspirations, expectations to God and substitute
trust for magic. Rather, we constantly put Yahweh to
the test: "If you do this for me, then I will believe in you.
If you do not do it, I will doubt your goodness." Thus,
parents, shaken to the roots by the birth of a retarded
child, may be strongly tempted to question the goodness
of God. Such a temptation is understandable, but if we
attempt to impose on Yahweh a reduction of his covenant
by crying out for the elimination of a specific personal
anguish, then we have become idolaters. We have made
a certain relative good—admittedly of tremendous importance to us—an absolute good. We are not accepting

Yahweh's promise of love; we are rather imposing conditions on him. We are telling him what behavior we insist on as appropriate. We have, in effect, created a graven image for ourselves, for we are postulating a God who can be subject to our demands. Such a God has nothing to do with the Yahweh of Sinai. If the very heavens cannot contain him, if the whole physical universe cannot contain him, how do we expect to contain him with our conditions, requirements, and stipulations?

These are tough words, but I don't see any way to escape them. We either believe in Yahweh or we don't. If we do believe in him, then our lives have to be lives of total trust, no matter what goes wrong—even death. Eventually, as Charles de Gaulle once remarked, we "shall not fail to die." Death itself is a relative evil compared to the absolute strength of God's love.

Jesus repeated this prohibition of idolatry when he pointed out that the Yahweh who provided for the birds of the air and the flowers of the field would certainly provide for us. Jesus did not, obviously, guarantee the elimination of human suffering; all he assured us was that God's love was more powerful than any suffering and would eventually triumph over it.

This is very hard to believe, but then no one ever maintained that it would be easy to believe Yahweh or Jesus. It is much easier to deal with a God on whom we can set some minimal conditions, one who will in return for certain services rendered by us guarantee some stability and reliability in our lives. Such a God would be a comforting, responsible, reasonable God. And when all is said and done, this is the God with whom most of us deal most of the time; but we must face the fact that if that is the God we want, we might just as well forget about the Israelite and the Christian religions, for the God of the Sinai myth and the God of the Jesus myth is not that kind of God at all. In his self-revelation, he is the only absolute; everything else, all human aspirations and enterprises, are relative. That is a terribly arrogant position for him to take, but once we understand who he claims to be, then we are forced to admit that any other posture would be a denial of what he is. A God you can deal with is a nice cozy God, but he is really no God at all.

I am not, be it noted, an anti-institutionalist. I am committed to the Roman Catholic Church and value deeply its religious traditions. Even though I am appalled at the corruption and incompetence of many of its leaders, I still believe that it will persist all the days, even unto the end. I am also convinced that for all its weaknesses and ineptitudes, it is the only community in which I can encounter the God in Jesus. I am also convinced that it is the best community for encountering Jesus. But once all these things are said, it seems to me that every Roman Catholic who is true to the best of his own tradition must assert that the organized Church structure is a means and not an end; that many of us, especially leaders, but followers too, have turned it into an end; and that is not only idolatry, it is a perversion of the best of the Catholic tradition.

Heaven protect us if the only way Yahweh can work in the world is through the ignorant and incompetent men who are Church leaders—indeed, there is a long record of ignorance and incompetence dating back to the beginning. Any church made up of human beings runs the risk of being presided over by incompetents most of the time. Our faith does not depend on the intelligence of our leadership (for which thank God!). But both those who feel constrained to assert that incompetent leadership is good leadership and those who spend all their religious energies fighting incompetent leadership are in fact idolaters. In both cases, something relative—indeed, quite relative—has been made absolute.

The hierarchy has no monopoly on idolatry. We are told, for example, by some young people that unless the Church takes a vigorous stand on racial justice, they will not think that Christianity is worth believing in. I think the Church should seriously condemn injustice. I also deplore the past failings of the Church in racial matters, and I applaud the zeal of young people to improve racial relations in our country. I am outraged by what has been done to black Americans, and I think it is time to eliminate bigotry, discrimination, and prejudice from our society. But having said all these things, I must insist that the crusade for racial justice, no matter how holy, how admirable, how morally excellent, is not a religious absolute. The only religious absolute is God; and to make one's response to God dependent on the ethical stands of the Church is idolatry.

Similarly, many Catholics are extremely excited about new movements in the Church. For some of them their religious lives have become centered in sensitivity training or pentecostalism or the cursillo movement or, more recently, various attempts to link Christianity with the occult. Each of these movements may have considerable wisdom in them; each may be admirable; each may merit a good deal of our religious attention. But when any becomes the center of our religious life, when any becomes our absolute religious concern, then we have made for ourselves a graven image, and we have reduced our relationship with God to a technique, a method, a formula.

The Church's record in dealing with women is abominable. One of the canons of the present code of canon law equates women with children and idiots. The hundreds and thousands of women religious in the world are governed by a number of antiquated Italian gentlemen in Rome. Although it certainly has nothing to do with the essence of our doctrine, we have for scores of years insisted that woman's place is in the home—and many of us still insist on this despite John XXIII's endorsement of feminism. We use the most absurd reasons to defend the prohibition against women priests. For all these reasons (and more), the feminist movement in the Church is critically important; but it is no substitute for God. Nor is denouncing the Church's stand on birth control a substitute for God. Nor is any movement, activity, commitment, interest, or concern a substitute for God.

I am speaking of the practical order of our everyday lives. In theory, we are all perfectly willing to admit that feminism, racial justice, peace, birth control, pentecostalism, clerical celibacy, sensitivity training are not at the center of our religious commitment. But for all practical purposes, most of the time we so readily live as if those perfectly legitimate but relative interests were indeed absolute. They preempt our emotional concerns, they demand all of our vital energies, they occupy most of our "religious time." Theoretically they may be recognized as relative, practically they have become absolutes.

One good way to test ourselves is to ask how much of our "religious" conversation is devoted to these issues and how much to God's love? And if the truth be told, most of us are at perfect ease in talking about the latest "relativity" in our religious life; we are not in the least bothered by recounting the latest faith healing or tongue-speaking experience in our pentecostal group. We are not at all embarrassed when it comes to talking about the Church's discrimination against women. We are absolutely confident when we talk about the immorality of racial injustice. Then when it comes time to talk about God, we stumble, we are vague, we express doubts and bafflement; and in all likelihood we say nothing at all—mostly we have nothing to say because we have not thought much about the subject. We have been too busy, in other words, dealing with the really important things.

The last of the golden calves was not the one Moses destroyed.

The religious and devotional and social issues with which we are concerned are important. I would argue, however, that they are only appropriate for members of a Yahwistic religion when they are pervaded and transformed by a commitment to and a consciousness of the powerful, loving God who is at the center of our religious life and in whose ultimate goodness and triumph we have complete trust. One can tell whether a man is an idolater not by what he does but by the way he does it.

Some commentators see in the first sentence of verse 5, Chapter 20 of Exodus a statement of liberation. Yahweh is freeing his people from idols. There is no need to bow to or serve lesser deities. Man is now free to enter a covenant with the real God as a partner and not as a slave. No concern, no commitment, no cause is important enough to reduce us to slavery. If we yield ourselves over to a movement in such a way that the movement dominates us, then we are not only idolaters, we have become slaves. Yahweh no more wants us to be slaves than he wants us to be idolaters. Only if we have a conviction of the ultimate graciousness of the universe are we sufficiently confident of ourselves, of our own goodness and the goodness of creation, to be involved in a movement and still sufficiently detached from it so that it does not dominate us. It is absolutely impossible for a Yahwist to become fanatic. A fanatic is a man dominated by his cause. A pretended Yahwist who permits a cause to dominate him has departed from the covenant with Yahweh to sink into idolatry. There have been a lot of fanatics in human history who identified their causes—no matter how noble—with Yahweh; that identification is idolatry and slavery. Those of us who choose to be fanatics had better beware, for Yahweh our God describes himself in the second sentence of verse 5 as an impassioned God. Passionate people tend to be intolerant of idolatry, hypocrisy, and phoniness.

The words used in verses 5 and 6 to describe the quality of Yahweh's relationship with his people are extraordinary. It would only be in much later years that prophets like Hosea and Jeremiah and Ezekiel would make explicit use of sexual imagery to describe the relationship between Yahweh and his people. Those who first set down the Decalogue and those who added the commentary contained in verses 5 and 6 (commentary which, incidentally, is apparently on verse 3 as well as verse 4; hence, on the whole revelation, not merely on the prohibition of graven images) did not choose to develop the covenant symbol into a marriage symbol. It was perhaps because of their fear that such symbolism would be easily confused with the fertility symbolism of Israel's neighbors. It was only in later years, after Yahweh was firmly established as the Lord of fertility, that his relationship with his people could be described in sexual imagery. When Jeremiah and Ezekiel used such imagery, they minced no words:

The word of Yahweh was addressed to me saying:

If a man divorces his wife
and she leaves him
to marry someone else,
may she still go back to him?
Has not that piece of land
been totally polluted?
And you, who have prostituted yourself with so many lovers,
you would come back to me?—it is Yahweh who speaks. (Jeremiah 3:1)

The Lord Yahweh says this: For having undressed and let yourself be seen naked while whoring with

your lovers and with your filthy idols, and for giving
them your children's blood—for all this, I am going
to band together all the lovers who have pleasured
you, both those you liked and those you disliked, I
am going to band them together against you from all
ground; I will strip you in front of them, and let them
see you naked. (Ezekiel 16:35–37)

Verses 5 and 6 of Chapter 20 of Exodus indicate that
if the marriage symbol was not implicitly present in the
covenant symbol, then at least the vocabulary used to
describe the covenant would almost inevitably give rise
to a later sexual symbolism. For example, the word *hesed*,
which means "an overflowing of kindness and love" describes an extremely intimate human relationship. In
Hosea's description of the relationship between himself
and his prostitute wife—a symbol of God's relationship
with his unfaithful people—he says, "I will betroth you to
myself for ever,/betroth you with integrity and justice,/
with tenderness and love"; (Hosea 2:21). It is the word
hesed that is here translated as "tenderness."

The word "love" in verse 6 of Exodus 20 is *'ahabah*,
which can mean "to desire," "to breathe after," "to love,"
"to delight in." It is, for example, the word that is used to
describe the relationship between the sexually aroused
bride and groom in Chapter 2, verses 2–3 of the Song of
Songs:

—As a lily among the thistles,
so is my love among the maidens.
—As an apple tree among the trees of the orchard,
so is my Beloved among the young men.

And the word that our text translates as "reject" is
sane, which can mean "feel a sexual revulsion." (See 2
Samuel 13–15.) Thus, when the people turn away from
Yahweh, they are behaving like a wife who turns away in

disgust from her husband's aroused and passionate tenderness and his desire to make love. The "guilt" of verse 5,
Exodus 20 is a translation of the word *awon*, which means
"twisted" or "bent" or "distorted." A wife who rejects her
husband's love is abnormal, frigid, sick, perverted.

Thus, Yahweh offers his people tenderness and demands
an aroused response to that tenderness. Those who turn
away in revulsion from his tenderness are perverted, and
those who respond with openness and trust he will shower
with affection. For he is *el kana*, which we usually translate (even in the Jerusalem Bible) as "a jealous God." It
is more appropriately translated by the text of the Hebrew
Torah we are using in this book as "an impassioned God."
Yahweh is involved, passionately involved, with his people.
He offers them wildly passionate love, and dismisses as
perverted those who turn away in revulsion from such
love.

This analysis of the words in verses 5 and 6 indicates
that what is being described is not a God who is eager to
work judgment on his people but rather the statement of
a passionate, aroused lover.

In later years, Israel's religious thinkers began to use
explicit sexual imagery to describe the covenant love; but
this religious development was relatively minor compared
to the original development in which Yahweh was described as entering a personal relationship with a people.
Once the relationship was conceived of as a I-Thou inter-
action in which God became passionately involved with
his people, it was a logical step to compare the covenant
to a marriage.

The thought of Yahweh lusting after the body of his
bride will be offensive to many prudes and puritans. What
the imagery attempts to convey, however, is the fact that
human sexual arousal is a relatively weak emotion compared to the passion of God's love for his people.

Those who will be offended by the imagery will be

inclined not to take the imagery seriously. There is something undignified about a God who permits himself to be described as "lusting for his creatures." In addition, it is also incredible that God should pursue us with a passionate tenderness the way the groom pursues the bride in the Song of Songs. We may even applaud the imagery as being beautiful, but still refuse to live lives in which we really believe that the Ground of Being, the Ultimate, the Absolute, or *ipsum esse,* as we used to call him familiarly in the days of scholastic philosophy, really relates to us as a passionate lover. Beautiful symbol, yes, but scarcely one that can be taken literally.

But what must be said is that to the extent the symbol is inadequate, it is meager rather than excessive. It does not describe Yahweh's love passionately enough. Sexual arousal may be the most powerful and pervasive positive emotion that a man can experience. It is an inadequate description of Yahweh's love; his passion for us is not less powerful but rather infinitely more so.

There is another implication of the sexual imagery of the Old Testament. A relationship between a husband and wife is constantly in a state of evolution and development. It has its ups and downs, its successes and its failures, its excitements and its discouragements. No man or woman with any experience of marriage expects instant perfection in the relationship. Nor does any couple really think that their marriage can reach such a state of perfection that no further growth or development is possible or required. Surely, the relationship between Yahweh and his people corresponds to this phenomenon of marriage as a developing relationship. The words in Ezekiel and Jeremiah that we quoted above show how much trouble and conflict there was in the love between Yahweh and his people.

If we think of our relationship to God as rather like marriage, we then understand both the need for constant development and also the inevitability of discouragement and setback. We are caught in a relationship with a passionate God; he does not demand perfection of us; he does not demand a smooth course in the relationship; he does not demand that we eliminate all failure or even all infidelity from our lives. What he does demand is that we continue to respond to his love. Faith in Yahweh does not generate religious perfection; it merely generates a determination to keep trying. Commitment to Yahweh is not the end of faith, it is only the beginning. The convinced Yahwist is not the perfect man, nor even necessarily the good man; he is, rather, the man who has taken a certain existential posture vis-à-vis the deity and has committed himself to working out his life possessed by his conviction of the validity of the symbolism of a passionately aroused God. The Yahwist believes that he has been "caught up" by such a passionate God, and he tries to live a life which demonstrates response to such passion. But he understands that far more important than the perfection of his response is the fact that he continues to respond no matter how strong the discouragement or how many the failures.

There are, then, two issues. The first is, do you believe in a God that corresponds to the Yahweh symbol? Secondly, how passionate is your life as a response to the God so symbolized?

In individual human beings the answers to these questions are tangled and confused. Our faith is always weak and shabby. Yet, in the midst of lies and indecisions, hesitancy, doubt, and equivocation there is frequently to be found a solid kernel of faith, a faith which many times seems to exist almost despite ourselves. We may have surrounded ourselves with all kinds of idols; we have done everything we can to blur the issue, to beg the question, to avoid the challenge. Yet there is still a part of our being that believes and responds and loves.

What is important for all of us is not to judge the extent

of the faith or the response of others but to look honestly at our own faith and response. As I examine my own heart, I know that I accept, indeed, with a powerful intellectual conviction, the idea of a passionately gracious universe; but I must be wary of becoming too confident over that conviction, for I am by training and temperament an intellectual—someone who deals with words and ideas. For me to "accept" an idea and to develop it into "conviction" is not all that difficult an exercise. What I must doubt is whether that intellectual conviction pervades very much of the rest of my being.

I proclaim that the fundamental religious issue is not the Church or birth control or the philosophical and historical problems of interpreting the Old and the New Testament myths. I insist, rather, that the central question is, do the Jesus and Yahweh myths describe a gracious Reality to which I am prepared to commit myself? I also announce, at least implicitly, that I have made such a commitment. And yet, whether my life is pervaded by trust, joy, hopefulness, and a "radiation of graciousness" is a question about whose answer I must remain extremely skeptical. I am one of those who spent his earliest years in the midst of the Great Depression, a time filled with both the general tragedy of those years and the special ones in my own family. When I see movies of the little boy I was before the disaster of the Depression, I am astonished at what a joyous, spontaneous little child he was. I have to go the very depths of my own consciousness to find even a trace of that joy remaining.

Seriousness, diligence, responsibility (why else would someone write so many books?), a sober, at times grim dedication to work—these are the realities that have filled my life as long as I can remember. What else does one do, after all, when one has unconsciously accepted responsibility for the Great Depression?

But is is very difficult for a child who has taken on

such an awesome responsibility to live a life of passionate and joyous romance with a gracious God. His intellect may say one thing, but his primal, semi- and unconscious emotions say something quite different. After all, the Depression may come back.

I am not saying these things to justify my own inadequacies as a Christian. However, mine are the only inadequacies that I feel qualified to discuss. One could come to the issue of adult religious commitment with better experiences than mine, but, Lord knows, one could also face the question of the graciousness of being with far worse ones. Each of us, in other words, has a past to transcend. We have inclinations of personality both genetic to the human race and specific to our own experience that make us very hesitant about the leap of faith and commitment required to surrender ourselves to the *hesed* of the *el kana*, the loving tenderness of a passionate God. Our fight against these tendencies does not end when we make an intellectual commitment to that God. On the contrary, the fight has just begun.

But then part of the commitment involves the belief that our fears and our hesitations, our built-in personality weaknesses and neurotic distortions will not, in the final analysis, be overcome by our efforts. They will eventually be swept aside by the *'ahabah*, the aroused love, of God.

CHAPTER 7

THE NAME OF THE LORD

You shall not swear falsely by the name of the
LORD your God; for the LORD will not clear one
who swears falsely by His name. (Exodus 20:7)

Verses 7 and 8 of Exodus 20 in the Torah, are the second
and third commandments in the Catholic tradition (in
other traditions, the third and fourth). They are, in a
sense, transitional commandments. Verses 1–6 of the twentieth chapter of Exodus are essentially a description of the
kind of God that Israel encountered in the desert. Verses
12–14 shape the broad context of the moral behavior
deemed appropriate for a Yahwist. Verses 7 and 8 are
both religious and moral. They set down certain proscriptions, but they are of secondary importance compared to the religious truth which motivates them.

The Catholic who grew up in the years before the Vat-
ican council cannot help but be surprised when he begins
a serious study of the text of Chapter 20 of the book of
Exodus. It turns out that in most cases things we thought
the commandments forbade are either a minor part of
what the text really means or have nothing to do with
the intent of the text. We believed, for example, that the
second commandment regulated the use we made of the
names of God and Jesus and also forbade "dirty" lan-

guage, which included everything from "damn" to the scatological and the obscene. The differences between profanity, scatology, and obscenity were never very clear. They were all lumped together in our consciousness under the category of "bad language" or, alternately, "swearing." I remember one good nun seriously arguing that to say to another, "Shut up," was a violation of the second commandment.

This peculiar hangup was not unique to us. Apparently the proclivity of late Judaism to substitute "Adonai" for "Yahweh" in the text of the scripture also resulted from a misreading of this commandment.

In its original context, the commandment meant something very different. What it prohibited was the misuse of religion, a misuse based on the same assumption that led men to build idols. Just as the idol gave the worshiper some control over the god, so in the ancient world the use of the name of a god gave one control over the deity. Thus, if one used God's name, one had God at one's disposal. Idolatry is forbidden in the first commandment, magic is forbidden in the second; for neither by the use of idols nor by the use of God's name can we control what Yahweh does.

In the ancient world, a man's name represented his reality, his essence (if we may be permitted the use of the scholastic term). When you named something, as did Adam in the garden, then you dominated it, controlled it, because you had grasped its reality. As Martin Noth says, "Anyone who knows a divine name can make use of the divine power present in the name to effect blessings and curses, adjurations and bewitchings and all kinds of magical undertakings."[1] Men were told that God's name was Yahweh in order that they might praise him and call upon him, but not that they might use that name for frivolous purposes, for God's name is his pres-

[1] Martin Noth, *Exodus*, op. cit., p. 163.

ence, his *sehenah,* his glorious majesty in our midst. Yahweh is the Lord of creation, the mover of history, the
passionate lover. To try to use his power and his presence
for silly or trivial purposes is an insult, and he who
misuses religion for unreligious purposes is a hypocrite.
The phrase that the Torah in our translation renders as
"will not clear" is the verb *yenakeh,* which can also
mean "will not be proclaimed pure or innocent." Another
way of putting it, then, is "He who invokes religious power
for frivolous or trivial purposes will be deemed a hypocrite." There is no more scathing denunciation of hypocrisy in the Old Testament than that to be found in
Amos 5:21-25:

> I hate and despise your feasts,
> I take no pleasure in your solemn festivals.
> When you offer me holocausts,
> . . . . (line missing)
> I reject your oblations,
> and refuse to look at your sacrifices of fattened cattle.
> Let me have no more of the din of your chanting,
> no more of your strumming on harps.
> But let justice flow like water,
> and integrity like an unfailing stream.
> Did you bring me sacrifice and oblation in the wilderness
> for all those forty years, House of Israel?

What Yahweh is seeking from his people is not a vain
and foolish approach to religion but a righteous one. Since
the word "righteous" is used frequently in the Israelite
religious tradition to describe both God and the people,
it is appropriate that we determine what the word means.
Needless to say, it does not mean righteous in the sense
of "self-righteous," as it is usually used today. The righteous person is upright, serious, responsible, sober—not in
the sense of being dull, but rather in the sense of reacting
with appropriate seriousness to serious events. The He-

brew word for righteous is *zedek*. In its primary sense it means "one who is judicially vindicated," but the judicial vindication presumed that the person was originally innocent and that his claim was just. A righteous judge is one who awards the verdict to an innocent defendant; he is a man who behaves appropriately in the circumstances in which he finds himself. He is an upright person in the sense opposite to the *awon* or person twisted in the sense described in the last chapter.

In our contemporary vernacular, a man of *zedek* is "straight" or "sincere." He is not a phony; he enjoys integrity and credibility. To use *zedek* of Yahweh, then, means that he is the sort of God you can count on, you can trust; he means what he says, he is a responsible, reliable God who possesses both integrity and credibility.

A people who have *zedek* are serious, mature, and responsible in their response to Yahweh. They deal with him as he has dealt with them. They do not use religion for frivolous purposes; neither do they pretend to a religious superiority they do not possess. Professor Williams raises the question of why Yahweh's threat is against those whose religion is trivial or frivolous:

> But why the terrifying threat? Why include here the stern admonition when no such admission follows, for instance, the sixth commandment? Precisely because this commandment is so easily broken. Murder, adultery, theft, and the like are overtly willed acts. Even belief in other gods is usually a conscious deed. Hypocrisy in religion, however, can begin almost without notice. We can use God's name irreverently without even realizing the deed has been done. Therefore it is particularly necessary to remind the believer of the consequences.[2]

[2] J. G. Williams, *Ten Words of Freedom*, op. cit., p. 139.

And the consequences of frivolous and hypocritical religion are not so much consequences Yahweh wills as the inevitable consequences that vain religion brings upon itself. For if religion is converted from an end to a means—and that is what this commandment is about—then Yahweh disappears. What we have left may be magic; it is certainly no longer religion.

The late social psychologist Gordon Allport in his researches on the various dimensions of religion shed considerable light on vain and frivolous religion. Allport was fascinated by the finding that those who seem to be most religious on a number of measures of religiousness (such as church attendance) were also the most likely to score high on measures of prejudice, discrimination, and bigotry. He began to wonder how it could possibly be that those who professed faith in a gracious and loving God could themselves be so ungracious and unloving in their relationships with others. He proceeded, then, to develop a social-psychological instrument which measured (at least in its initial forms) two "dimensions" of religiousness: the intrinsic and the extrinsic. Those who were extrinsically religious "used" religion. It brought them peace of mind, reassurance, security in dealing with the problems of everyday life. Those who were intrinsically religious viewed religion not so much as a way of acquiring peace and security but rather as a means of opening themselves out to the world and to their fellow men. Not surprisingly, Allport's research demonstrated that it was only the extrinsics who were prejudiced. Those who professed an intrinsic religion were the least likely of all his respondents to be bigots.

I remember a meeting convened by a Jewish agency to discuss research it had commissioned (by two gentile researchers) on religiousness and anti-Semitism. These two worthy scholars had discovered, not surprisingly, a correlation between religiousness and anti-Semitism. They

had not, however, taken Allport's theory into consider-
ation nor used his scale to discriminate between intrinsic
and extrinsic religion—an omission that most of the social
scientists in the group felt was an incredible display of
professional incompetence. But some of the Protestant and
Catholic social actionists present at the meeting would not
accept a distinction between intrinsic and extrinsic religion. As one of them pointed out to us, "You can't define
your religion the way you want to. You're stuck with those
who are extrinsically religious and you've got to assume
responsibility for them."

Of course he was quite wrong. Any religion does have
the right to determine what style of religious behavior is
expected of its members. In the Yahwistic tradition, extrinsic religiousness is hypocrisy and vanity. Yahweh will
not render a judgment of innocence or cleanliness on
those who use religion as a means to obtain personal security. If Yahweh will not assume responsibility for the
extrinsically religious, there is no reason why Yahwistic
religion must assume responsibility for them. Unquestionably, some of the behavior that has gone on in the churches
may have reinforced extrinsic religion, though I think most
psychologists would agree that the roots of extrinsic religiousness are to be found in childhood relationships with
parents and not in one's early or later encounters with a
church. If it turns out that those who are intrinsically
religious do indeed accept Yahweh on his own terms and
are also more inclined to racial prejudice, then Yahwism
is in deep trouble. If it is not only those who pursue religion as a means of finding peace and security who are
bigoted but also those who open themselves out in response to a gracious universe, then Yahwism is a fraud.
But neither Judaism or Christianity causes prejudice. On
the contrary, when they are taken seriously they eliminate
it. The problem is not that authentic Yahwism can coexist
with prejudice, for it cannot. The problem is that many of

us who profess to be followers of Yahweh do, in fact, use his name in vain, convert his worship into other purposes, and, while professing faith in Yahweh, in fact we are narrow, frightened, insecure, bigoted human beings. I suppose the churches can probably be faulted for not doing all they can to facilitate people's development out of this narrow, extrinsic, magical, frivolous approach to religion. But the failure then is of religionists, not of the religion. It is a failure of those who follow Yahweh but who do not take him seriously rather than of Yahweh himself and those who do take him seriously.

The religion of Yahweh is not intended to be a formula, a how-to-do-it technique for solving problems and achieving emotional security. One need only walk through any religious bookstore to see several shelves filled with how-to-do-it religious books. Such volumes purport to provide either the wisdom or technique for achieving salvation. Simply by purchasing and reading these books we can become faith healers, pentecostals, Buddhas or yogis, satanists or Jesus freaks, Christian radicals or masters of extrasensory perception. We can learn about alchemy, reincarnation, enhancement of our sexual lives through Yoga, charms, potions, and spells. We can cover how to obtain the truth from the I Ching or the Tarot cards or the study of macrobiotic diets.

In many of these manuals, there are grains of truth. But one truth most of them seem to miss is that salvation is not a matter of technique or formula, of special skills, or of gnostic wisdom—at least it isn't in the Jewish and Christian traditions. Yahweh promises us his love and the confidence and peace that go with possessing that love. He doesn't promise us peace of mind and soul, added sexual potency, personal security, and success in business or the elimination of worry and anxiety automatically from our everyday lives. Religion is not a way of achieving self-fulfillment, personal maturity, or satisfying human relationships. The man of faith obviously has powerful motivations to break out of the fears and insecurities and anxieties that stand in the way of maturation and adult relationships, but Yahwism is no substitute for psychotherapy and psychotherapy is no substitute for Yahwism. Yoga may, for all I know, be an interesting and useful technique; it has no more to do in itself with authentic response to Yahweh than did the Nine First Fridays or the Sorrowful Mother Novena or the recitation each day of fifteen decades of the rosary. These devotions could have been authentic. For many people they did in fact represent an opening forth in trust to a gracious God and an ultimately benign universe. For others, they were religious techniques designed to produce personal security and confidence in one's own value and worth. Salvation does comes from Yahweh, but it comes as a gift and is accepted in faith. It can be neither earned nor guaranteed by any technique or method hitherto devised. Neither the speaking of tongues nor the going on pilgrimages, neither devotion to Our Lady of Perpetual Help nor extrasensory perception have of themselves anything to do with a serious response to a serious God. Such devotions may for some people be a serious response—so may concern about ESP. There is a place for gimmickry in human life, and there is a place for technique and method in religious development, too; but technique does not guarantee us salvation and cannot pretend to give us peace and confidence. Salvation is a gift of the Lord that has already been given, and peace and trust come only from the acceptance of that gift. Techniques and methods are useful for developing the self-discipline necessary to live lives of gracious and trusting response. They are ways we overcome the residues of fear that still impede us from being joyous followers of Yahweh.

As long as I live, I will need to make constant effort against the morose and melancholy proclivities of my personality. On the other side of the coin, it will require never ending self-discipline for me to be able to live in such a way that the remains of the frolicsome leprechaun that I was in my earliest years can come more and more alive. I therefore am constrained to learn as much as I can about how to combat the neurotic and frightened aspects of my personality. I must adopt forms of self-discipline to focus my energies so that the part of me that responds best to Yahweh can become more and more typical of the person my friends and colleagues encounter.

But such formulae, methods, techniques, and insights are no substitute for faith and no guarantee of the peace that comes with faith. If I attempt to convert my painfully acquired wisdom and self-discipline into the center of my religious behavior, then I have become guilty of the religious frivolity and vanity that this commandment forbids. For what Yahweh wants, unaccountably enough, is not my efforts but me. It does not follow that my efforts are worthless or that Yahweh condemns them. On the contrary, I daresay he expects them, but if I am not confident enough of Yahweh's love to believe that he delights in me even when I am grim and morose, then all my efforts toward greater wisdom and greater self-opening are not at all superior to the sacrifices and burnt offerings so roundly denounced through his spokesman Amos. My righteousness comes not from my own efforts but from Yahweh who made me and loves me. My efforts must continue, but as a consequence of Yahweh's love, not as either a substitute for it or a cause of it.

It is difficult to understand why from Yahweh's point of view our most serious, dedicated, painful efforts are vain, frivolous, and trivial. Rushing blindly through divine office, rigidly making that half-hour meditation before Mass every morning, conscientiously reciting the stations of the cross every day during Lent, weighing that last ounce of lunch so as not to violate the fast, or, more recently, standing on our heads in some contorted yoga posture—all these are difficult and painful, and Yahweh doesn't give a damn about them. If we are Jewish, we may choose to keep all the dietary regulations; if we are Islamic, we may choose to make pilgrimage to Mecca; and if we are Catholic, we may, depending on our particular stance at the moment, say the rosary and go to Mass every day or speak with tongues at a pentecostal meeting. Splendid. These may be acts of great virtue on our part. There is nothing wrong with them. On the contrary, there may well be much that is right with them. But such activities guarantee nothing. Any peace and security we obtain from them has been gained as a result of a vain and frivolous use of religion.

It is very hard to understand that in our relationship with Yahweh the only thing that really counts is our response to his love.

A while back, I was asked by the New York *Times* literary supplement to do a lengthy book review on some fifteen paperback volumes on "the new religions." I could not help but conclude that Yahweh stood in a very poor competitive position compared to the gods of the how-to-do-it manuals. There is something very reassuring about a technique or about a form of wisdom that somehow or other is an "inside secret." Compared to the sure-fire technique for the hidden wisdom, Yahweh has little to offer. Those whose religious lives absolutely require security and the safety that comes from a technique or a formula had better stay away from Sinai. There isn't any technique to be learned there, nor any wisdom that has been hidden down through the ages. What was offered at the foot of Sinai was not a method but a covenant, not a how-to-do-it manual but a demand for a trusting relationship with a passionate, almost crazy God. Small wonder that the how-to-do-its are selling so well.

CHAPTER 8

THE SABBATH

8 Remember the sabbath day and keep it holy. 9 Six days you shall labor and do all your work, 10 but the seventh day is a sabbath of the LORD your God: you shall not do any work—you, your son or daughter, your male or female slave, or your cattle, or the stranger who is within your settlements. 11 For in six days the LORD made heaven and earth and sea, and all that is in them, and He rested on the seventh day; therefore the LORD blessed the sabbath day and hallowed it. (Exodus 20:8–11)

Of all the commandments the one demanding the holiness of the sabbath day is the one that most befuddles the scholars.* It is generally agreed that nobody knows for sure what the origins of the sabbath custom are. There can be no doubt that other tribes and peoples in the ancient Middle East kept some sort of seven-day cycle. However, the seventh day was apparently a taboo day, a day when bad spirits were abroad, and it was risky to

* The reader should be reassured that I am not working on this chapter on Sunday. Indeed, I have taken a solemn resolution that I shall never again work on a book on Sunday—well, at least not unless it is absolutely essential.

attempt any work. The sabbath was perhaps in its origins an evil day in which nothing was done for fear that the demons would fight or destroy what man had done. The custom had the obvious social function of providing rest for both slaves and animals, and it may well be that enlightened rulers used the seventh-day superstition as a pretext for easing somewhat the burden of those who had no means of protecting themselves. In the theological explanation contained in verses 9, 10, and 11, there is a trace of this, for not only are the Israelites to be free from labor, so are their slaves, the strangers among them, and even their cattle. In the version of the Decalogue contained in the book of Deuteronomy, the point about lifting the burden of slaves is emphasized:

> Remember that you were a slave in the land of Egypt and the LORD your God freed you from there with a mighty hand and an outstretched arm; therefore the LORD your God has commanded you to observe the sabbath day. (Deuteronomy 5:15)

If Israel was freed from its slavery by the Lord in the land of Egypt, so it should at least reach forth its arm on one day and free its slaves and servants and strangers in the camp from the burden of work. As Professor Williams puts it with his characteristic elegance:

> Israel is called to celebrate the Sabbath as a reminder of her freedom from slavery, which God wrought through the Exodus. Each Sabbath day should be marked by a return of that feeling of glorious relief experienced as Israel crossed the Sea of Reeds. Israel is called to rejoice, their days of servitude are over, and to consider with compassion the servitude of others.[1]

[1] J. G. Williams, *Ten Words of Freedom*, op. cit., p. 151.

But obviously the whole context is now changed. The sabbath may be a day of the mysterious and the uncanny. It may also be a day in which burdens are lifted, but the uncanny is now not frightening or threatening and the burdens are lifted not because of fear of taboo, not because the sabbath is an unlucky day, but, on the contrary, because it commemorates the luckiest event in the history of Israel: its encounter with Yahweh. The sabbath is a holy day, a day on which Israel rests from its work so that it may engage in other activity and celebration.

We have no idea from the sources available to us how this transformation came about. The sabbath custom was part of the religious "baggage" that Israel carried with it into the desert. In the transforming experience of the Sinai encounter, the sabbath was transformed too, indeed, almost stood on its head, and fused into the new religious synthesis. Israel now rested not out of fear but because of delight. The sabbath was the day of the week set aside to experience in a special way the ongoing encounter between Yahweh and his people. It was not a time of major covenant renewal, for that took place, at least in the early days, only every seven years; but it was a time when the joys of the covenant were recalled more explicitly than they were during the rest of the week.

The sabbath, then, became part of history. It was a recollection and a celebration of a past event, but also a re-creation of that event. While in its origins it may have been part of some natural cycle (though it is difficult to link a seven-day week with a lunar month), in Israel's case the sabbath day was torn from the natural context and given historical importance. It was no longer part of the fixed cycle of the universe; it had become involved in Yahweh's saving intervention in human events. It re-created the past and it directed the way toward the future.

Whatever the origins, then, of the sabbath custom, for Israel it became the Lord's day. As Rabbi Heschel in his beautiful book *The Sabbath* puts it, "Sabbath is one of life's highest rewards, a source of strength and inspiration to endure tribulation, to live nobly. The work on weekdays and rest on the seventh day are correlated. The sabbath is the inspirer, the other days the inspired."[2]

Heschel points out that as a religion of God's intervention in history,

> Judaism is a *religion of time*, aiming at the *sanctification of time*. Unlike the space-minded man for whom time is unvaried, iterative, homogenous, to whom all hours are alike, qualitiless, empty shells, The Bible senses the diversified character of time. There are no two hours alike. Every hour is unique and the only one given at the moment, exclusive and endlessly precious.[3]

Heschel adds, "The Sabbaths are our great cathedrals"; the Sabbath is a day of *menuha,* a day of happiness, stillness, peace, and harmony. Heschel quotes the ancient catechism as saying, "What was created on the seventh day? Tranquility, serenity, peace, and repose."[4]

The Sabbath is not a day when one is forced to cease all human activity. Heschel says, "The Sabbath is a reminder of the two worlds—this world and the world to come. It is an example of both worlds: For the Sabbath is joy, holiness, and rest; joy is part of this world, holiness and rest are something of the world to come."[5]

The Sabbath provides the same *menuha* as does Yahweh the shepherd offer calm in the green pastures, for the "still waters" are called *menuhot*. It is beside these peaceful waters that we sit in repose on the Sabbath. The

[2] Abraham Heschel, *The Sabbath: Its Meaning for Modern Man.* New York: Farrar, Straus & Young, 1951, p. 22.

[3] Ibid., p. 23.

[4] Ibid., p. 22.

[5] Ibid., p. 19.

ancient rabbis even called the Sabbath "the Bride," "the Queen" because it was the most glorious and beautiful event of their lives.

Heschel says, "On the Sabbath it is given us to share in the holiness that is in the heart of time . . . eternity utters a day."[6] He describes the relationship of the Sabbath to the rest of human life as follows:

> Six days a week the spirit is alone, disregarded, forsaken, forgotten. Working under strain, beset with worries, enmeshed in anxieties, man has no mind for ethereal beauty. But the spirit is waiting for man to join it.
>
> Then comes the sixth day. Anxiety and tension give place to the excitement that precedes a great event. The Sabbath is still away but the thought of its imminent arrival stirs in the heart a passionate eagerness to be ready and worthy to receive it.[7]

Then the Sabbath candle is lighted and "just as creation began with the word 'Let there be light,' so does the celebration of creation begin with the kindling of lights."[8]

> And the world becomes a place of rest. An hour arrives like a guide, and raises our minds above accustomed thoughts. People assemble to welcome the wonder of the seventh day, while the Sabbath sends out its presence over the fields, into our homes, into our hearts. It is a moment of resurrection of the dormant spirit in our souls.[9]

There is no doubt about the sublimity of the themes developed by Rabbi Heschel, and while such themes are

[6] Ibid., p. 65.
[7] Ibid., p. 65.
[8] Ibid., p. 66.
[9] Ibid., p. 66.

surely not explicit in Exodus 20, they are legitimate conclusions from it. If the sabbath is a holy day, a day
blessed and hallowed by the Lord, and if, as Deuteronomy says, it is a day that commemorates the Lord's
bringing Israel out of Egypt, then it is a day when people
experience the peace, the tranquillity, the joy of special
contact with the Lord. It may have taken some time for
Israel to come to the understanding that the holiness of
the sabbath was the same as the holiness it encountered
at Sinai, but once that connection was made, the insights which Heschel summarized were inevitable.

And it surely seemed legitimate for Yahweh to ask for
a day for himself. If he had made covenant with his
people, then his people surely owed him at least one day
of the week when they could explicitly reflect on the
covenant and commune with him in loving acceptance of
his graciousness. It also made sound psychological sense.
It was easy to forget about Yahweh unless one day was
devoted to him. Furthermore, a God who didn't demand
at least one day out of seven of his people's lives could
not, after all, be that much interested in them. Finally, a
God who sanctified time by his own intervention in human events could easily seem to disappear from time unless he had a day to himself. The sabbath was the day
of Yahweh, signifying both the commemoration of Israel's
encounter with him in the Exodus and on Sinai and also,
eventually, in anticipation of the Day of Yahweh when
his work would be accomplished with the coming of the
eschatological age.

Of course, legalism raised its ugly head, and what became important on the sabbath was not so much the joy,
tranquillity, serenity, and peace, not so much the contemplation and reflection, but rather the avoidance of
work. The laws, the regulations, the details imposed to
make sure that no work was done ceased to be a means
and became an end in themselves. Jesus was not the only

rabbi to denounce vigorously those who became so concerned about the letter of the sabbath that they no
longer understood this particular day. The denunciations
of Jesus and other rabbis did not eliminate legalism, as
the specifications of our theology books of not so long ago
made clear. They carefully determined just how much
work on Sunday resulted in serious sin and how much
omission of Mass was necessary so that it would have to
be repeated. The ultimate absurdity (for me, at least)
came in a theology class where we were told with a perfectly straight face that crocheting was not sinful on
Sunday but knitting was (I think it was that way, but for
all I remember now, it may have been the other way
around).

The result of such legalism is that the sabbath is ignored by an ever increasing number of people. Many if
not most Jews feel that it is impossible in modern life to
keep all the requirements of the sabbath observance
(though increasingly some of the sabbath ceremonies are
returning to Jewish family life). The servile work regulations of the old moral theology were so absurd that they
have been thrown out the window by most Catholic
clergy and laity. Furthermore, Catholics are beginning to
take the same attitudes toward Sunday churchgoing as
do their Protestant brothers. It's a nice thing to go to
church if you want to, but one is certainly not going to
hell for all eternity if one decides to sleep late. Some
serious younger Catholics, in fact, insist that they will
happily go to Mass one day a week, but not on Sunday,
both because Sunday Mass is a drag and, besides, no one
has the right to tell them what day they have to go to
Mass. Finally, in certain aggressive Catholic circles, the
decision to "drop out" of Sunday Mass observance "because I don't get anything out of it" is taken to be a badge
of how enlightened and advanced one really is. Sunday
Mass, in other words, may be all right for superstitious

pre-conciliar Catholics, but it is scarcely required for so-phisticated, "modern" Catholics.

Anyone who reads through Rabbi Heschel's profoundly moving pages can readily see how all this is beside the point. Those who drew up the servile work regulations and who insisted that if you came in before the creed you did not have to repeat Mass but that if you came in after you did not only misunderstood the nature of Yahweh's love for us, they also misunderstood the whole purpose of the sabbath.[10]

Sunday is the day when the Lord our God comes to us. It is a day when our more frantic activities should grind to a halt so that we may have the peace, the tranquillity, the serenity to commune with our God, to reflect on our lives, and to renew our covenant of faith and love with Ultimate Graciousness. One cannot do that by showing up in church for forty-five minutes on Sunday morning (or now, the night before). Staying away from the lawn mower on Sunday afternoon or venturing over to the parish church in the morning has nothing to do with a joyous celebration of the Lord's covenant with us; it has even less to do with a serene, peaceful, contemplative reflection on God's love and the purpose and meaning of our lives. We feel that once the "obligation" of Sunday has been honored, we are now free to engage in such undeniably important activities as poring through the Sunday newspaper, watching the pro game on TV, struggling through expressway traffic to visit places we don't want to, and all those other contemplative, reflective activities Americans do to "kill time" on weekends.

[10] I realize, of course, that the Christian service on Sunday is not quite the same thing as the Jewish observance of the sabbath. In the early Church, Jewish Christians kept both days for different purposes. In the larger sense, however, Sunday is obviously a continuation of the sabbath because it is the day consecrated to the Lord.

Indeed, as one of those many Americans who usually work a seven-day week, I was profoundly embarrassed by Rabbi Heschel's book. A whole day for reflection and tranquillity? What would I do? Surely, he doesn't mean that I should stop reading or writing or listening to football games? He couldn't possibly be insisting that during the summer I should give up wrestling with the wind and the waves in my *Leprechaun*. If I can't do these things or if I can't attend those critically important rituals of American society, the weekend conferences, what is there left for me to do?

Take tomorrow, for example. It is Sunday, the Lord's day, the Christian sabbath. I will certainly have to work on the next chapter of this book. I have to interview some teen-agers for an article I may write for *The New York Times Magazine*, and then, in the evening, I must give a lecture at the O'Hare Airport Chapel (never can tell when you're going to need help there), and, finally, I must prepare for what is going to be an extremely hectic week. Reflect? There won't be any time. Be tranquil? Not without the help of a pill. Serenity, peace, joy? What the hell are they?

If there is something obviously wrong with those who thought that sabbath joy and tranquillity could be imposed by precise legalistic regulations (be they Talmudic rabbis or moral theologians), there is something equally wrong with those who profess to be followers of Yahweh and find almost no time in their lives to commune with him. If we believe in a God of history, a God who intervenes in time and makes it holy, then how come we have so little time for him? How come we work so frantically, as though everything depends on how much we can squeeze out of time and nothing depends on how much he can put into time?

It is all the more surprising when one stops to consider that the amount of time most men must work in middle-

class American society is much smaller than that required of working men ever before in human history. We
manage to fill up our time, of course, and we manage to
fill up our expanding leisure with a wide variety of time-
killing activity. In the peculiar combination of university
and church that constitutes my environment, a seven-day
week is an absurdity. It is absurd not merely because no
one is requiring it of me (save occasionally) but because
after four or five days of productivity, one really has
nothing left to produce; tranquillity and reflection are
really the only meaningful alternatives—unless, of course,
one must run away to another nutty conference. I find
things with which to fill up my weekend for the same
reason other people do: if there weren't such things, I
just wouldn't know what to do with myself. It would be
nice if we could take a few minutes or a few hours of our
time on a Sunday afternoon to reflect on Yahweh's leading Israel out of Egypt and entering into covenant with
them at the foot of Sinai, or even possibly, just possibly,
to reflect on the risen Jesus to whom Sunday is supposed
to belong. That would be very nice, but there isn't any
time for it.

I am not talking of moral obligations, and I certainly
do not advocate a return to a puritanical "blue laws"
approach to the sabbath. I am saying that those of us
who profess to believe in a God intervening in time and
directing history ought to be able to devote a little more
time—our time and our history—to religious reflection and
tranquillity. Obviously, it doesn't have to be done only on
Sunday, and obviously there are going to be some Sun-
days in our lives when it cannot be done. The point is
that Sunday is as good a day as any and probably better
than most. (Save for parish priests in parishes which,
unlike the one I live in, have large Catholic populations.
For the typical American diocesan priest, Sunday will
never be a day of reflection and tranquillity. One must

say Mass, preach, distribute Communions, and, above all, count the money—not much time for serenity in the midst of all that!) Sunday is the day when most of us do not work and it is the day which is traditionally thought of as "the Lord's day." I have no suggestions as to what *must* be done on the Lord's day, and I certainly am in no position to exclude the National Football League from the list of appropriate behavior; but I think the sabbath has to be approached from another viewpoint than from the perspective of "what must I do" or "what must I not do."

The appropriate question to ask ourselves on Sunday evening is, do I approach the beginning of the new week with more serenity, tranquillity, joy, and faith than I was conscious of last Friday evening? If the answer to that question is not yes, if we have had no experiences throughout the weekend that deepen our faith, that heighten our religious sensitivity, that bring a little bit more of tranquillity and serenity into our lives, then religiously speaking the weekend has been a waste and we must wonder whether we really believe that our God is a God that sanctifies human time. If we believe that Yahweh has made covenant with us, that Yahweh is to be experienced not merely in certain places but also, and more especially, in the development of human events through time, then we must face the fact that certain times belong to him. If he does not have certain segments of our time as specifically his, then our consciousness of him will simply fade away from all other segments of time.

My colleague Martin Marty has suggested that our weekends away at the "second home," which is becoming a part of middle-class life, may spell the deathblow for Sunday observance. He may be right, but I would like to rephrase the problem. The question for the churches is not how to get people to go to Mass when they are away at their summer homes or out in the country camping or engaged in some other frantic effort to get away from it all with large groups of other people who are also trying to get away from it all; I think the question is, do we have enough faith and confidence in the goodness of God really to trust ourselves to relax? We must address ourselves to the human and religious problem of discovering satisfying, rewarding, taxing, tranquilizing, challenging uses of the tremendous amount of new leisure time we have available. Most of the compulsive behavior during leisure time in American society (and I include here my own compulsions) is the result of the fact that we feel guilty when we aren't doing anything. If tranquillity generates guilt, then we certainly have no time to deal with Yahweh. Oh, of course we will go off to pay our respects to him on Sunday morning in church; but that's *doing* something. A time of reflection, contemplation, prayer, spiritual and personal growth? Well, that's not *doing anything*. The stern Protestant ethic, which infects most Americans, warns us that we must do something, even if it's only going over to turn on the TV to watch a Charlie Chan movie that wasn't very good when it was made in the 1930s. Any activity, in other words, is better than having to face ourselves, and, of course, if we cannot face ourselves, there isn't much hope that we can face the Lord our God.

It will be hard for religious leaders to persuade their people that some of the new leisure time must be used simply to slow down and to reflect. Slowing down and reflection are not only absolutely essential prerequisites for prayer, they are also in themselves an act of faith and trust, a manifestation of response to Yahweh's graciousness. We will have a hard time persuading the people of this because obviously we do not believe it ourselves. There are meetings to go to, events to be planned, and, yes, even books to be written.

Religious leadership that is unable to acquire some tranquillity and serenity, that does not bear witness to its faith in the gracious God by finding some time to relax and reflect, and does not permit serenity to permeate at least some of its time is in no position to condemn a compulsive, materialistic society. Nor does it have any legitimate complaint when its parishioners venture forth on the expressways on Friday night looking for serenity and tranquillity some other place besides the parish church.

Let me put the matter as bluntly as possible. If we who are Yahwists, clergy or laity, do not believe strongly enough in a trusting, gracious God who has entered into an intimate and passionate relationship with us, then it is very dubious that we will ever find time for peace, joyfulness, and celebration in our lives. There is certainly a strong question as to whether we really believe in the Yahweh whom we profess to honor. The third commandment is part of the covenant to the extent that those who really honor Yahweh, who have really entered into covenant with him, will not only have no trouble devoting some of their time to him, but will wait eagerly for those moments when the Sinai covenant will be renewed.

CHAPTER 9

CHILDREN AND PARENTS

> Honor your father and your mother, that you may
> long endure on the land which the LORD your God
> is giving you. (Exodus 20:12)

With the fourth commandment we turn to the more specifically ethical components of the Decalogue. I have argued as the basic theme of this book that the twentieth
chapter of the book of Exodus represents not so much a
moral code as an account of a religious experience. The
covenant symbol describes an encounter between Israel
and Yahweh, and the Decalogue is part of the ancient
covenant form. The principal stipulations of the covenant
between Yahweh and his people are contained in the first
two and possibly three of the commandments (or the
first three and four of the commandments, given the
Jewish way of numbering them). The essential stipulation of the Decalogue is that we should respond with love
to Yahweh's passionate love for us. The more explicitly
ethical stipulations contained in commandments four to
ten (five to ten in the Jewish numbering) ought to be
interpreted in the light of the covenant symbol and the
religious experience that that symbol manifests to us.

My colleague John Shea has pointed out to me that
there is a danger in the approach to symbol interpreta-

tion that both he and I use. Christians can view the religious symbol as a "truth to be applied." The symbol will be taken as an intellectual statement from which certain conclusions are to be drawn, and then these conclusions are to be lived out in our lives as evidence that we understand and believe the symbol. Yahweh has made covenant with us; therefore, we will engage in certain specified behavioral activities as evidence that we believe in the covenant and are honoring it in our lives.

I think Father Shea's point is well taken. It would be very easy to regard verses 12–14 of the twentieth chapter of Exodus as a concrete, practical application of verses 2–11. In the first section of the chapter we are told the truths we believe in, and in the second section we are told the practices in which we must engage. This approach to religion has so permeated the Catholic tradition for so long that none of us are really immune from it. It is very difficult to extirpate it from our religious lives.

But this is not what is expected of us at all. A man who gives himself over to a religious symbol, who accepts it as a guiding and illuminating force in his life, does not so much "apply it" to his concrete behavior as he "puts it on," makes it a perspective, a viewpoint, indeed, a set of eyes through which he views the world. A religious symbol is not applied, it is embraced. One does not deduce certain specific modes of action from it. On the contrary, one immerses oneself in it and discovers what the world looks like from within a commitment to the religious symbol.

A proper approach, then, to the second half of the Decalogue is not to see it as application of the first half but rather to ask ourselves how, once we have accepted the idea of Yahweh's gracious covenant with us, that idea will affect our behavior with our fellow men. The issue is not what kind of things we are required to do for our parents and what sort of things we don't have to do. The appropriate approach is to ask how relationships between parents and children look when both parents and children believe in the graciousness of a covenanting God.

The fourth commandment as we presently have it is obviously aimed at adults, so it is describing not the relationship between young children and their parents but rather that between adult children and their aging parents. The instruction given does not so much require obedience as it does "honor." Indeed, the literal translation of the Hebrew word would mean "give weight." That is to say, Yahweh tells his followers that they will treat their aging parents with honor and reverence and respect. And he promises them that if the parents are reverenced and respected they will "long endure on the land which the Lord your God is giving you." It is generally agreed that the Lord is not so much promising that as a special added extra reward he will grant long life to those who honor their aging parents. Rather, he is asserting that honoring the aged is a necessary prerequisite for a healthy and successful society. There are two passages in the Old Testament which develop in more explicit detail the respect owed aging parents. The first is Leviticus 19:3: "You shall each revere his mother and his father, and keep My sabbaths: I the LORD am your God," and the other is Ecclesiasticus 3:1–16:

Children, listen to me your father,
   do what I tell you, and so be safe;
for the Lord honours the father in his children,
   and upholds the rights of a mother over her sons.
Whoever respects his father is atoning for his sins,
   he who honours his mother is like someone amassing a
     fortune.
Whoever respects his father will be happy with children of
   his own,
   he shall be heard on the day when he prays.
Long life comes to him who honours his father,

he who sets his mother at ease is showing obedience to
    the Lord.
He serves his parents as he does his Lord.
Respect your father in deed as well as word,
    so that blessing may come on you from him;
since a father's blessing makes the houses of his children firm,
    while a mother's curse tears up their foundations.
Do not make a boast of disgrace overtaking your father,
    your father's disgrace reflects no honour on you;
for a man's honour derives from the respect shown to his
    father,
    and a mother held in dishonour is a reproach to her
    children.
My son, support your father in his old age,
    do not grieve him during his life.
Even if his mind should fail, show him sympathy,
    do not despise him in your health and strength;
for kindness to a father shall not be forgotten
    but will serve as reparation for your sins.
In the days of your affliction it will be remembered of you,
    like frost in sunshine, your sins will melt away.
The man who deserts his father is no better than a blas-
    phemer,
    and whoever angers his mother is accursed of the Lord.
(Ecclesiasticus 3:1–16, Jerusalem Bible)

In the Leviticus segment there is emphasis on the legal
role of the father and the mother. They have certain
"rights" over their children. But Ben Sira, the author of
Ecclesiasticus, makes a rather different case, and one
which may be more in keeping with the spirit of the
Decalogue. We are to help our parents in old age; we
are not to humiliate them; we are to respect them; we
are to be kind to them, because this is the sort of behavior that will guarantee us a good reputation in society
and also a similar response from our children when we
become old.

There is a good deal of psychological insight in Ben

Sira's rather worldly-wise advice. As we deal with our parents, so our children are likely to deal with us—not because of any extrinsic religious judgment on us but rather because our children will learn from us how we deal across generational lines. If the self-indulgent heroes and heroines of contemporary "youth culture" have such contempt for their parents, the reason may very well be that they have learned such a model of appropriate trans-generational behavior from the contempt their parents had for *their* parents. If old people are shunted aside into nursing homes, treated with impatience and contempt in the house, and deprived of the opportunity for any useful or productive contribution to society, then the children of these aging people should not be surprised when *their* children treat them with equal contempt, even though that contempt may be displayed over different issues and different fashions. Today's youthful radicals, so filled with hatred for the failures of those "over thirty," could well ponder the fact that these attitudes and styles of behavior toward their predecessors will become an in-grained part of their personalities, which will undoubtedly rub off on their own children and guarantee similar ha-tred from them. He who does not respect and reverence his parents will not be respected and reverenced by his children. The habits of one generation are visited upon another generation, not so much by religious guilt as by powerful mechanisms of personality development and psy-chological socialization. No matter what our parents say to us, the way they treat our grandparents will shape our attitudes toward them, even if they and we are un-aware of it. In a society where there is little respect or reverence for the elderly, children will certainly have lit-tle respect for the middle-aged. Children who are yet unborn will someday do to their parents precisely what is being done to parents today.

Obviously, not all American adults treat their aged

parents with contempt. Furthermore, most young people are not of the youth culture and do deal with their parents in a respectful and reverent fashion (a respect and reverence which is not obscured by extreme casualness of style). But there is a strong tendency in American society to disregard the old (and you are old today, I am afraid, after your forty-fifth birthday). That tendency will guarantee an equal tendency for young people to write off all those over thirty as worthless sellouts, from whom nothing important can be learned.

The fourth commandment requires compassion. It declares that in a society without compassion for the aged, there will not be enough trust or respect for the society to persist long. One of the most atrocious vices of our time is that of selective compassion. We worry about those who are dying in Vietnam (and we certainly should) but we worry little about our own aged. We demand sympathy and understanding for the blacks as they strive for equality in American society (and indeed we should), but we are rather less likely to require sympathy and compassion for ethnic middle Americans or for middle-aged liberals or for the men who fought in the Second World War who still believe that there are things to be said for patriotism. Some points of view are to be considered with every possible allowance made for the context in which they are spoken, and other points of view are to be judged rigidly and harshly without any regard for the context in which they are spoken. For some groups we must make every possible allowance and try to understand their behavior in the context of all the excusing factors that may be at work; others are to be written off as guilty without any such allowances made. Collective guilt is imposed on whole bodies of people, and all their members are to be judged guilty until proven innocent, while in other cases even individuals clearly guilty of obvious crimes are to be excused because of what "society has done to them." Furthermore, it is absolutely imperative that we have scapegoats and that guilt and blame be distributed among them with all the care and precision that is possible.

There is an incredible amount of arrogance, rigidity, and intolerance in this effort to determine who is guilty and who is innocent, who must be excused and who must be blamed. It is not enough that a society discovers where mistakes have been made, lies been told, and even where individual immoral actions were committed; guilt must be distributed up and down across the length and breadth of the society, and everybody must be made to confess guilt and to expiate their sins.

Under such circumstances, of course, there is little room for universal compassion or sympathy. Whole generations are written off as guilty, with the only question being, who is more guilty and who is less guilty? It is necessary that sins be punished and even then they are not to be forgiven.

Well, that is one way to run a society, I suppose, but in any human community where a number of people have appointed themselves inquisitors to hunt out and punish the guilty, trust and compassion vanish. If all whites are racists, then there is no reason for black people to try to enter relationships of sympathy and compassion with whites. Many Americans—probably more white than black —would argue that trust between whites and blacks is impossible, and they would also argue that trust between the old and the young, the rich and the poor, the educated and the uneducated is impossible. If this argument is proclaimed frequently enough, it may become a self-fulfilling prophecy. If compassion and trust disappear from a society, the social environment will become a jungle.

It is decreed, in effect, that everyone must become like us—the "us" being whoever is issuing the decrees. Social peace and harmony will be established not by learning how to live with those who are different from us with some kind of trust and respect; it will come rather from eliminating differences, from everyone's sharing the same values, the same perspectives, the same interests, and the same commitments. There is no room for diversity, we are told, in a modern democratic society.

This is nonsense of course. A peaceful society comes not from the elimination of diversity but from the integration through conflict, compromise, and trust. A mature adult is not someone who demands that all others adjust themselves to his values; he is secure and confident in his own values and is able to deal with respect and integrity with those whose values are different.

It is very difficult to put up with those who are different from us. Most of the conflicts in human history have been fought over rather small differences of language or skin color or nose shape or eating habits. He who is different is not to be trusted. If he is given the opportunity he will do us evil, therefore we do evil to him before he can do it to us. The incredible massacres in Bangladesh were worked by one Muslim group on another, with the only difference between the two groups being that one had somewhat lighter skin than the other. Even a common religion, then, cannot prevent massacres among populations who are slightly different from one another.

It may be extremely difficult to live with diversity, but it does not follow that we can eliminate it or that we should seek to. The fourth commandment tells us, as I understand it, that we must learn how to live with those who are different from us and look upon them with respect, tolerance, honor, and patience. Yahweh demands that we have compassion for those who are not like us.

Following Father Shea's advice and trying to put ourselves within the covenant symbol and look at the human phenomenon of the conflict that comes from diversity, what light does that symbol shed on conflict and diversity?

It is very hard to answer this question. Traditional theology has seen human diversity as the result of original sin and has argued that were we without sin there would be one race, one language, one nation, one religion. It has always seemed to me that this argument is absurd. While much of the evil in the world has come from human diversity, so have almost all the riches of human culture. It would be a sad, dull, monotonous world if everyone was like everyone else. In addition, even if we could eliminate diversities of language, creed, and race, we would still be faced with the fundamental diversities of sex, age, and intelligence.

It seems to me that from the point of view of the covenant symbol a number of things can be said about diversity. First of all, Yahweh loves all men. Even if his initial covenant was with Israel, it was made with them because they were a priestly people, who were to bear witness to Yahweh's love to all other nations and eventually to be a channel for Yahweh's salvation to the nations. If Yahweh loves everyone, then young must love old, white must love black, poor must love rich, hardhat must love hippie, Republican must love Democrat, and Saxon must love Celt.

But I think more than that must be said. If Yahweh loves them, then there must be something good in them, and those things which are different in them exist not as a threat to us but for our education, our enlightenment, and our enjoyment. The diversity of the world's peoples is the result of Yahweh's plans to enrich human life. It is a great splendid joke he had played on us, a joke which, alas, we have been too dull and dense to understand.

The most important point of all is that if we really believe in Yahweh's loving graciousness, then we can afford to be lovingly gracious to others. I take it that this is the fundamental principle of Yahwistic ethics. We are able to love others because we have strength and confidence in God's love for us. We do not have to be suspicious or distrustful or afraid of others because we know that Yahweh will take care of us. We can offer ourselves in open, trusting relationships to those who are different from us because they are no ultimate threat to our existence. There is nothing they can do to take from us the most important thing in our lives, God's love for us.

Obviously, we have a long way to go before such trust and confidence becomes typical of relationships among individuals and nations, and there are no simple short cuts on the path to a world that is free from suspicion and hatred.

Compassion becomes possible when we no longer have to fear others, and Yahweh's covenant dispenses us from fear. It does not make life easy; it does not eliminate social conflict; but it does assure us that no threat, however powerful, can destroy the core of our being, which is in a permanent and indissoluble covenant with the Lord our God.

It becomes possible, then, in the narrow instruction of this commandment to honor one's aging parents because, even though they may be difficult and demanding, even though they may stand for different values, even though their ways may not be our ways, still they are in no way a threat to us. They are of no danger to us; there is nothing really important that we have that they can take away, at least not permanently. There is conflict between generations, of course, and there always will be, just as in human society there is likely to be conflict among the different racial, religious, and ethnic groups. But conflict need not mean mutual destruction, nor need it exclude sympathy and compassion. All human relationships, even the most intimate and loving, are marked by ambivalence.

Faith in Yahweh cannot eliminate ambivalence, but it does make possible the honest recognition of it, which is the only necessary prerequisite for mature love. It also makes possible compassion and sympathy in the midst of conflict.

There is relatively little compassion in the world, not much sympathy, not much ability to tolerate diversity, and relatively little honoring of aging parents. But the reason for these phenomena is not that Yahweh's command has not been heard; it is that we have never yet had enough faith to give us the strength and the courage, the confidence and the trust to honor the commandment.

CHAPTER 10

OUR FELLOW MEN

You shall not murder.
You shall not commit adultery.
You shall not steal.
You shall not bear false witness against your neighbor.

It is interesting to ponder the fact that but one verse of the twentieth chapter of Exodus in the Torah sums up the four commandments that occupy most of the space in our catechisms and our moral theology books. We spent one whole semester in our seminary years on *de justitia* and another whole semester on the course *de sexto*.[1] Such an expenditure of time seemed reasonable, for obviously it was the sixth and the seventh commandments, and to a lesser extent, the fifth and the eighth, which were the really important ones. Most sins that were committed were against these commandments (and it was no secret, of course, that the sixth commandment was most likely to be violated). It never occurred to us that it was rather peculiar that the really important commandments were all found in one verse. We never asked why Yahweh spent so much time talking about unimportant things like strange gods and so little time talking

[1] Which meant, of course, "concerning the sixth commandment," not sex.

about adultery or theft. We were, of course, only too willing to make up his mind for him and establish extremely complex rules as to what sort of thievery was "mortal" sin and what sort was "venial" sin. Even more elaborate systems were established determining how, when, and where we were to make "restitution" to others for violating the seventh commandment. Among the things we learned, for example, was that if we burned down Peter's house, intending to burn down Peter's house, then we had to pay "every last cent" toward rebuilding that domicile. But if we burned down Peter's house thinking it was Paul's house, we were not bound to restitution to Peter because we didn't intend to harm him. It didn't make much sense then and it makes less sense now.

I am not saying that regulations regarding human property are unimportant, though I am inclined to think that in a society like ours, they might more appropriately be left to lawyers than to theologians. Nor am I prepared to say that there are no moral issues in sexual relationships; clearly there are (though there may be religious and theological issues of greater moment than the quantities of female anatomy which may be displayed without committing more than a "venial" sin).

The fundamental criticism to be leveled against the old moral theology is not that it was frequently absurd in its casuistic conclusions. Its basic flaw, rather, was that it thought it was the business of religion, and particularly of Yahwistic religion, to lay down specific guidelines for human behavior that would have universal application independently of time and space. I do not believe that any serious moral theologian at the present would argue that the details of an ethical code can be deduced from the Christian symbol system. On the contrary, even in the old days most of our moral argumentation fell back upon the so-called "natural law." But our "natural law" was not quite the same as it had been for Cicero or even Thomas Aquinas. It was not what most people in most times and most places thought was appropriate behavior; it was rather what moral theologians and papal advisers thought ought to be moral behavior for all people in all times and all places. "Natural law"—in the sense of traditional human wisdom—is the basis of all ethical systems (even if the frequently hated phrase "natural law" is not used). But if ethics is the result of natural human wisdom, then a revelatory experience of God ought to add nothing in particular to the wisdom that the race already possesses. It may have been appropriate for future priests, deeply involved as they would be in assisting people to make agonizing moral decisions, to be well informed about the various traditions of ethical wisdom, but to treat that wisdom as something that could be deduced from Israel's experience of Sinai in the desert or the early Christian's experience of the risen Jesus was both to falsify the experiences and to trivialize the arduous work of ethical reflection.

There are, as I will argue in a later chapter, very strong ethical implications of the covenant symbol. But these implications neither add to nor subtract from human ethical wisdom. What they do, rather, it seems to me, is prescribe a certain style of behavior, a certain approach to human problems and human decisions which will mark the man whose being is permeated by the religious symbol to which he has given himself. There is not a necessary difference in the concrete programmatic response of a Jew and Christian on the one hand and a pagan on the other to a given problem of social injustice. The covenant symbol does not provide any better insight into the nature of the problem or necessarily any better solution for it. The difference between the Yahwist and the pagan is to be found in the *style* and *manner* with which they approach the problem and the people involved in it.[2]

In the post-Tridentine Catholic Church, it was not perceived that the basic contribution of religion to ethical decision was a style of behavior and not a detailed set of moral answers. The answers grew more and more elaborate and more and more detailed, and yet they could not keep up with the appearance of ever more complicated problems and ever more splendid opportunities for sin. The moral theologians tried, heaven knows, and each year the "Moral Guidance Notes" in

[2] Since I accept Schubert Ogden's principle for the verification of religious symbols, I must assume that the validity of the covenant symbol is to be tested by its ability to "re-present" in a most powerful way the fundamental assurance man has from the very structure of his being about the purpose and worth of human existence. The covenant symbol, then, reinforces a primordial and very hesitant instinct that all men have, that Reality may be gracious and even—however inchoately it may be felt—that love is at the core of the universe. Thus, it is altogether possible for a pagan and a Yahwist to have not merely the same programmatic response to a social problem but also the same stylistic and attitudinal approach to it. What the Yahwist brings that the pagan may not have quite so fully is a powerful explicit religious symbol that underwrites, reinforces, strengthens, and confirms the appropriateness of the response style. Or to put the matter more concretely, the Yahwist has a much more powerful symbol that demands of him universal human love. This may not seem to make a very great deal of difference. Why would a man's behavior be especially unique simply because his core religious symbol demands more explicitly and more powerfully the universality of love? One, however, need only inspect the human condition to see how little universal love there is. One may develop the understanding that all men are to be loved as one loves oneself without having the Yahwistic symbol, but the symbol is still of tremendous importance, as becomes obvious when we observe the behavior of that relatively limited group of men who have given themselves over completely to it. Furthermore, anyone who thinks that the nature of a man's explicit central religious symbolism is not important to his behavior simply does not understand the powerful and pervasive influence of symbol systems on human activity.

the Jesuit journal *Theological Studies* revealed the erudition and intelligence of those theologians who strove
desperately to keep up with man's skill at inventing new
sins.

They kept falling more and more behind, and questions of abortion, artificial insemination, "test tube
babies," the death penalty, war, foreign policy, racial
justice, stealing government papers, advertising, political
propaganda, the environment, population staggered the
most resolute moral theologians. Even in the serenity of
the pre-conciliar Church, they were necessarily falling
further and further behind in their codifications of "the
Catholic answer."

If the moral theologians are not as sure as they used to
be, editorial writers, columnists, political activists, college
professors, ecclesiastical bureaucrats, and Jesuit poets are
only too willing to provide detailed and specific instructions about what the only possible moral response to a
given problem should be.

If anyone can draw back a moment from the controversy that rages about these critical ethical issues of
our time, a number of things become apparent: First,
there are many inconsistencies in moral positions. For
example, militant Catholics who are deeply affronted by
abortion seem rather less concerned about napalm and
free-fire zones in Vietnam. On the other hand, the good
liberals who are horrified at the deaths of already born
children in Vietnam are not apparently very much concerned about the deaths of fetuses in the twenty-fourth
week of pregnancy. Those who are concerned about
abortion being legal murder are not terribly troubled by
the death penalty, nor are they much disturbed by the
horrors of the American penal system. Some of the American Irish are quite properly outraged by the British
treatment of Catholics in Ulster, but they lost no sleep
over Bangladesh. The brutality of some police forces is

rightly condemned, but there is little concern among many of those who protest the police behavior over the brutality of criminals who prey on innocent people, both black and white. Those right-wing political leaders who campaign on vigorous law and order tickets seem undisturbed by the thought that the most popular techniques for restoring law and order are the abolition of rights by which citizens are protected from oppression.

There is some reason to be suspicious about alleged moral wisdom that is not deeply concerned about its own inconsistencies. There is even more reason to be concerned about moral wisdom that attempts to substitute one form of rigid ethical requirement for another. Thus, those who argue (as did one Catholic psychologist in my hearing recently) that no one should have a child until after three years of marriage are as rigid and authoritarian as those who argue that everyone should try to have a child in the first year of marriage. Those enthusiastic supporters of feminism who, implicitly at least, assert that every woman should have a career are no more to be thought of as permissive than those who insist that every woman belongs in the home. Similarly, those who say that a woman should have absolute control over what happens to her body (an argument in favor of abortion) may not be much different in their simple approach to complex issues than those earlier Catholic theologians who argued that a woman had no control over what happened to her body.

There is a plenitude of simple solutions, of authoritarian regulations, of inconsistent and self-righteous rules of simple idiocy masquerading as moral wisdom.

In addition, there is an almost pathetic eagerness to believe that "things are changing," that, for example, as one article in *Newsweek* put it recently, "There is a burgeoning number of homosexuals." There may or there may not be more homosexuals. It may simply be that homosexuality is somewhat more public than it was in the past. One would think, to hear the celebrants of the sexual revolution, that pornography, adultery, and fornication were relatively recent developments in the history of the human race. It is possible that there were some major changes in sexual practices among college young people in the 1920s. Most of the research evidence suggests that there hasn't been much in the way of change since then, but one need only read some of the accounts of life in colonial America or investigate, even superficially, the sexual practices in those parts of the rural United States supposedly untouched by the influence of the mass media to realize that neither the Roaring Twenties nor the Radical Sixties have really developed anything particularly new in the way of sinfulness.

The real change is the emergence of a group of people —psychologists, counselors, student health advisers, and other "experts"—who attempt to persuade young people that promiscuity makes for personal growth. (They do so usually in the name of a very unsophisticated variety of Freudian psychology.) Such advice is used as an argument against the "rigid" taboos of the past. Rigid the taboos certainly were, and unhealthy too, for that matter, but it does not follow that there was not a kernel of very important wisdom contained within the rigidity of those taboos. William Shannon, writing in *The New York Times Magazine,* makes this point very well:

> Some modern parents are already so defeatist on sexual issues that they are having their 14-year-old daughters fitted with diaphragms or given prescriptions for the pill. But the powerful emotions surrounding the sexual act cannot be screened out as easily as the sperm. It is those emotions which young people have to learn to manage.
> Children of both sexes have to be taught what wise

mothers have always told their daughters, which is
that an intimate and important experience is cheap-
ened and coarsened when it is divorced from love.
If persons use one another like disposable plastic
cartons, the emotional content of the experience becomes comparably trivial. There are those who argue
that sex can be completely pleasurable even if one
barely knows one's partner or loathes him or her. I
would suggest that most young people are not so
tough or neurotic. Whatever they may protest to the
contrary, their feelings are engaged in the sexual act
and their feelings are bruised when it leads nowhere.

In sexual relations as in other areas of life, Americans have to relearn the satisfactions of self-denial
and anticipation. It would do no harm to 16- and 17-
year-old boys and girls to know the facts about sex
and yet not engage in intercourse. A certain amount
of frustration and tension can be endured—and with
good effect. Only modern Americans regard frustration as ranking higher than cholera in the scale of
human afflictions. An older, wise attitude regarded
self-restraint as a necessary part of becoming mature
and creative. But if our children are to learn how to
wait and how to discipline themselves, they will have
to acquire these habits long before adolescence.[3]

I am sure that most therapists of integrity and experience would be in fundamental agreement with what
Shannon says.

It is true that no one will go to hell or become unfit for
marriage because he or she has engaged in premarital
intercourse. It does not follow, though, that premarital
intercourse is a healthy, enriching experience. Much less
does it follow that one can detach sexuality from perma-

[3] William V. Shannon, "What Code of Values Can We Teach Our
Children Now?" *The New York Times Magazine*, January 16, 1972,
p. 52.

nent or quasi-permanent commitment without risking serious harm to selfhood.

I would argue, however, that norms regarding who sleeps with whom are more appropriate for ethics than theology. The Christian symbol system has better and different things to say about marriage than determining when enjoying the bustline of someone is not one's wife stops being venially sinful and becomes mortally sinful. Ethics cannot be divorced from religion completely, for ultimately man's view of what is Real has a powerful impact on his determination of what is Good; but a viewpoint about what is Good cannot be converted into a detailed ethical system without severe distortion.

I intend in this book vigorously to resist the temptation to engage in arguments about specific moral issues, for that would merely continue the mistake of equating the Sinai covenant with ethics and moral theology. I propose here, rather, a discussion of how those who accept the covenant symbol must make their moral decisions in an environment of incredible complexity, how one facilitates the development of "moral intelligence," and, in the next chapter, how this moral intelligence can be applied by nations. How does a man who has "put on" the covenant symbol respond to the dizzying complexity in which he finds himself?

There are, of course, many people who believe that it is immoral even to concede that there is complexity in ethical decision making. "I think it's a mistake," said a faculty member at an elite American university to me, "to tell young people how complicated social problems are, because complexity is an excuse for not being involved."

There are those who think that while a sophisticated and uninvolved student may be apathetic, an unsophisticated and involved young person may be a fanatic. There are even those who would prefer apathy to fanaticism. But the faculty member's comment neatly summarized two critical issues currently facing American higher education:

1. Is it possible to balance an awareness of the intricate complexity of social issues with moral commitment?

2. And, if it is possible to achieve such a delicate balance, has higher education any role to play in the development of such a balance?

The traditional stance of elite American higher education has been to shy away from questions of morality. One prominent college president has remarked, "There are two kinds of human development, intellectual and moral, and the college is only interested in the former." Furthermore, research scholarship has worked under a commitment to be value-free. Scholarship may indeed teach the virtues that are required for its own ends, but, whatever the scholar's own opinion, his scholarship is supposed to be neutral on other moral issues. Yet the youthful militants (and some not so militant) were incensed at what they took to be the immorality of their institutions and of many of their teachers. They demanded that colleges take moral stands that facilitate development of moral commitments in their students. Nor did the demands seem to be all that new. In a recent study done for the Carnegie Commission on American Higher Education by the National Opinion Research Center, it was discovered that the strongest predictor of satisfaction with their alma maters among alumni in their late twenties and early thirties was whether the college had contributed to the development of values and goals for life. One of the 1961 alumni—a Jewish businessman—summarized his feelings on the subject in very clear terms:

College is supposed to teach a person how to think and how to live. A person must learn the *meaning of*

life, and unless a person learns this he will be unhappy forever, and will probably make others unhappy. My college tried to mold my intellect, which
I have since realized is not man's most important
faculty. Man's spirit, his soul, is totally neglected by
college just as it is neglected by our materialistic
world, and as a character in "Karamazov" says: "Without God anything is possible." And now we are wit-
nessing the world crumbling around us simply because man has lost sight of his true essence, his soul.

I am very unhappy about the materialistic, money-
grubbing world I live in, but I am optimistic, because
the kids of today seem to have an understanding of
their essence and morality.

The problem of morality versus complexity is one of
the most knotty issues with which man has wrestled. If
one chooses in favor of complexity, then it would appear
that one must deny the relevance of general moral principles. On the other hand, if one commits oneself firmly
to morality, then there is the grave danger that reality will
lose its lamentable grayness and appear in tones of black
and white.

The liberal anti-Communists of the 1940s and 1950s, at
least in part because of their opposition to John Foster
Dulles' moralistic approach to foreign policy, emphasized
the complexity of political and social positions. Writers
such as George Kennan, Walter Lippmann, and Paul
Nitze came close to concluding that because of the subtle
and intricate nature of foreign policy problems, the nation had little or no choice but to base its positions on
what it perceived as its own most enlightened self-interest, since moral principles provided little or no practical
conclusions. Similarly, social scientists proclaimed "the
end of ideology" and seemed persuaded that most social
problems would yield to planning and technical competence rather than ideological visions. Finally, the ethical situationists insisted that moral decisions had to be

made in concrete circumstances, illuminated only by the overriding imperative of love.

But enlightened self-interest in foreign policy produced Vietnam; the unquestioned competency of the *Public Interest* school of social scientists did not in two liberal Democratic administrations notably improve the state of American society; and the imperative of love from the situationists did not modify relationships between white and non-white in American society. The people were lied to, some were oppressed, others were killed, students were dehumanized by the multiversity. Even though moral evil had been defined out of existence, it did not seem to go away.

The Movement was a swing away from complexity back toward morality. While situation ethics still reigned supreme on matters sexual, the young and their not-so-young admirers took vigorous moral stands on political and social issues. They did not hesitate to denounce roundly the liberal anti-Communists and those who spoke of the end of ideology as "immoral."

But just as an awareness of complexity uniformed by strong moral values could produce Vietnam, so strong moral values enlightened by an awareness of complexity produced the fanaticism of, let us say, the Weatherman faction of the SDS. Professor Kenneth Kenniston has pointed out in a number of articles how the student protesters have moral values which are much more autonomous and internalized than those of non-protesters. More recently Kenniston has added the observation that internalized morality by itself does not necessarily produce a balanced human personality. Other personality dimensions must develop at the same time as the moral value systems if the young person is not going to end up a highly motivated zealot.

And of zealotry we have had more than enough.

I am very skeptical of the enthusiastic moralist. The

men who murdered John Kennedy, Robert Kennedy, Medgar Evers, and Martin Luther King, Jr., all presumably thought of themselves as very moral men. We can dismiss them as insane bigots, but the step from single-minded moralism to bigotry or insanity is a short step. If I am forced to choose between Machiavelli and Torquemada I will cheerfully choose the former. The Machiavellis of the world have caused some human suffering and tolerated much more, but they are rank amateurs at creating human misery compared with the Torquemadas.

Nor will it help to argue, as do the disciples of Professor Marcuse, that my morality is better than yours and therefore you must adhere to my morality even if I have to force you to. Such an argument may have some short-range effect if he who poses it happens to enjoy more force than his adversary; but if he possesses less force, then he may find himself oppressed rather than oppressing; and if the force is relatively equal, the result is likely to be the blood bath of religious warfare. To be moralistic is bad enough, but to be moralistic about one's moralism is a guarantee of violence and tyranny.

But, surely, there has to be some middle course between Torquemada and Machiavelli. I am inclined to think there is, though, beyond doubt, he who tries to assume such a middle position often finds himself poised precariously on the edge of a razor.

Four propositions may be offered to define the limits of that razor's edge:

1. Even in the post-Freudian, post-Marxist age there are such things as good and evil. No matter how complex the issues, technical competence is not enough to arrive at decent and humane solutions. Dialogue between moral principles and technical complexity is difficult and intricate, but attempts must not be abandoned.

2. There are no simple answers to any of the problems

facing the American nation. To pretend that there are is to be irresponsible. Thus Professor Wald's response to the question of how the United States could withdraw from Vietnam "by land, sea, and air" was facile and witty but was not in the strict sense of the word a response at all.

3. Men of good will, intelligence, and complexity can agree on moral principles and still disagree on the application of these principles. To claim moral sanction for one's own solution and to repudiate others as immoral brings one dangerously close to fanaticism. Thus, most men by 1968 were agreed that the war in Vietnam should come to a speedy conclusion. Furthermore, some sorts of conclusions—thermonuclear war, for example—were clearly immoral, but, nevertheless, no single plan for disengagement was so obviously *the* right one as to be able to claim unique moral excellence. We may disagree and argue vigorously with those whose disengagement plans seem to us to be inadequate, but we ought to be wary of doing so in the name of the superior morality of our plan. Similarly, men of good will agree on the evils of racial injustice, but it does not follow automatically that, let us say, busing school children has a unique claim to moral excellence as a means of eliminating discrimination. Those who support busing may be able to marshal a telling case against those who oppose it, but the case is not so overwhelmingly clear to enable the advocates of busing to claim a superior *morality* for their position.

4. The intelligent and educated person is able to maintain involvement in social problems without becoming a fanatic. It is not necessary to have zealots in order that we might have reformers. Young people may have deep and permanent commitments to working for social change without needing to create scapegoats on which they can blame social problems.

Underlying these four propositions is the assumption

that there is a dimension of the human personality—which we will call moral intelligence—which can be developed in the maturation experience. This moral intelligence is not developed by faculty members who, as John McDermott puts it, see "themselves as embattled missionaries to the culturally philistine." It is rather, I think, the capacity to reexamine and clarify one's own values repeatedly in the light of concrete situations in which one finds oneself. Moral intelligence is the habit of not letting the picture of the complex gray reality which constitutes the political and social world be blotted out. The morally intelligent person is not satisfied with his own conventional wisdom, whether that wisdom inclines him to withdraw from problems that seem too complex or to charge into the problems which seem simple.

A classic example of moral intelligence at work was the behavior of the Kennedys at that point in the deliberations during the Cuban missile crisis when consensus had almost been reached for the bombing of Cuba. Attorney General Kennedy argued vigorously that such surprise attack was completely foreign to the traditions of the American republic. Characteristically, he asserted, "You're not going to make my brother the General Tojo of the 1960s." The issue was a complex political question and the solution to it was necessarily a political solution. One may disagree with that solution, but the point is that a far more dangerous and violent solution was averted, not so much in terms of political pragmatism (though surely there was an element of that) but in terms of a moral vision by which a nation had lived. One regrets that Mr. Kennedy was not present in 1965 to raise the same question when the decision was made to escalate the Vietnamese War.

The decision not to bomb Cuba is an excellent illustration of one of the peculiarities of moral intelligence. It is relatively easy for the morally intelligent man to know what not to do: He does not bomb Cuba, he does not get involved in a land war in Asia, he does not tolerate racial prejudice, he does not dehumanize college students. But it is much more difficult for him to know what to do positively to implement the values that are implicit in decisions about what not to do.

Can higher education make any contribution at all to the development of moral intelligence? I think it will not do so by direct and explicit effort. The thought of a course entitled "Moral Intelligence 101" is absurd and appalling. Equally appalling, but not so absurd, is the thought of faculty members subtly trying to convert students to their moral viewpoints, and, be it noted, these attempts of conversion are by no means limited to denominational colleges. I would suspect, rather, that moral intelligence is learned, if it is learned at all in a college, through interpersonal osmosis. Young people learn to exercise this virtue primarily because they have seen their teachers exercise it.

Faculty and administrators of a college, therefore, would contribute to the development of moral intelligence in their students by the following kinds of behavior:

1. They must demonstrate compassion for *all* people and not merely for those groups for whom it is currently fashionable to have compassion. Compassion for blacks is admirable, but so is compassion for Polish ethnics. When ethnics are discussed solely in terms of being a "barrier to social progress" they are not treated as human beings. J. D. Salinger's "fat lady"—even if she is Polish—is still Jesus Christ.

2. The faculty member or administrator must refuse to indulge in scapegoating as an outlet for his frustration. Blaming of individuals is great therapy for our Oedipal problems but it has nothing to do with either education or morality.

3. The campus adult will beware of reifying labels. Such catch phrases as "the Establishment" or "the military-industrial complex" or "the power structure" may be very useful political slogans but they are not accurate and precise descriptions of the reality of the social order. A faculty member may know that the Establishment is a myth but his youthful disciple may take it as a literal reality (only to be disappointed someday when he discovers that if there were an Establishment it would run things much more smoothly).

4. The faculty member or administrator will resolutely refuse to provide simplistic answers to complex questions. No matter how strongly he may feel about war or technocracy or race—and if he is fully human, he must feel strongly on all three—he will not betray his students by leading them to believe that all that is required to solve these three problems is common sense, moral righteousness, and enthusiasm. Furthermore, he will display proper reserve and skepticism about the latest fads and fashions in the academic world, no matter how strongly endorsed these fads and fashions may be.

5. The adult who is interested in the development of moral intelligence among the young people on campus will not hesitate to warn them that one of the most pernicious phenomena in the human experience is that mixture of guilt and self-righteousness which the late Ronald Knox once described as "enthusiasm."

In other words, if young people are to learn moral intelligence at all they will learn it from association with men and women who have strong moral commitments but who constantly are in the process of clarifying and revising their commitments, men and women who refuse to give up the struggle for a better and more humane world but who also refuse to impose their own contingent applications of moral vision on others as the only kind of authentically moral decency.

It is not easy to stand on the razor's edge between zealotry and apathy, but then it never has been. Perhaps that's why so few have tried.

We may have betrayed a whole generation of enthusiastic and idealistic young people by letting them believe that there were simple answers and that instant response to political activity was possible. Recently, a veteran (at twenty-six) student leader said to me, "My generation has lost on everything; we lost on the war, we lost on McCarthy, we have been excluded from the black movement, we've lost on educational reform, we've lost in the struggle against poverty. It looks like we will either have to make our peace with the system or turn to communitarian groups and a separate culture. Either way we won't have much impact."

The young man had much less self-pity than most students (though he certainly lacked the stringent honesty about himself that a Bernadette Devlin can display). He was not an extremist. He never had permitted himself too many illusions. Yet he was weary and worn. He seemed unaware that political and social change takes time, effort, and patience. He lacked faith that reform is possible, and he lacked the moral intelligence to understand that it is immoral to quit at twenty-six. Someone had failed to communicate to him the nature of the social reality in which man must live.

Again, a girl who had served a sentence in a federal prison on a narcotics charge commented, "The ones I really despise are the faculty. They had all their bright liberal fashions. They said it was all right for us to experiment with drugs, but they didn't have to go to jail and I did."

Finally, a student writing in criticism of the University of Chicago's student newspaper's stand on drugs asserted, "I am a pothead, an experienced tripper, a speed freak, and at one point I was mildly hooked on heroin. . . . I am not Levi [Chicago's president], I am not the fuzz, I am not Student Health; I am just a student, more screwed up than most, who earnestly hopes that somebody out there will profit from my unfortunate experiences. The sum total of my experience is that dope is bad. . . . I hate dope; but if I had my hands on an ounce of pure pharmaceutical cocaine, I would keep injecting it until it was gone or I was dead. . . . I just wish people in responsible positions . . . would think about the other side of the drug controversy."

I am not blaming the problems of these three young people on their college experiences. Presumably, much that went before the college years provided the roots for their difficulties. Nor am I arguing that the college should try to inculcate moral principles; it should not and probably cannot. Finally, I am not trying to defend the war, the administration, drug laws, or even the Establishment.

I am arguing that there are certain habits of mind which are an essential part of the disciplined intellect that enables one to approach moral issues with a sense of nuanced respect for the complexity of reality. If this respect is not to be found among many young people, the reason may be that it is not found among many of their teachers either.

CHAPTER 11

MORALITY AND FOREIGN POLICY

One of the most discouraging aspects of the moral complexity in which we find ourselves is that with all the good will and sincerity in the world, we still seem to make disastrous mistakes.

When I was growing up during World War II, my older friends who returned from the military repeatedly informed me that if we won the damned thing, the only reason would be that the other side made more mistakes than we did. Reading Liddell Hart's *History of the Second World War* in an accidental but bizarre counterpoint to the Pentagon Papers, I was forced to conclude that that judgment could be made not only of the Second World War but of most of human history, and, in any case, plowing through Liddell Hart and the Pentagon Papers is not an experience calculated to give one much confidence in the present condition of the human race.

Hart views the Second World War as unnecessarily begun and unnecessarily prolonged. Most of the great victories were more the result of the mistakes of the losing side than the genius of the winning side. Some of the most notable Allied triumphs, for example, were caused by previous Allied defeats which enticed Hitler to overextend himself.

Winston Churchill emerges from Liddell Hart as an inept blunderer. His ill-conceived campaign in Greece caused the English to lose the advantage they had gained in the western desert, and the consequent series of incredible disasters there were responsible for the fall of Singapore, as Churchill poured vast quantities of personnel and resources into each new blunder in the desert.

The casualties and destruction caused by stupidity on both sides were immense, and disasters like Hiroshima and Dresden are ample evidence that even in a war in which one side is engaged in legitimate self-defense, folly can lead to the worst kinds of immorality. A side which produced a "Bomber" Harris is in no real position to be critical of an Adolf Eichmann.

The men who inhabit the Pentagon Papers are remarkably like those who inhabited the Allies' side in Liddell Hart's history. They are guilty of immense folly, folly which it is as easy for us to recognize from hindsight as it was difficult for them to see at the time. Men make a mess out of things, not only evil and malicious men but also good and well-intentioned men, not only men of limited intelligence, like General Westmoreland and "Bomber" Harris, but men with very considerable intelligence, like Dean Rusk and W. W. Rostow. The human race is not very good at arranging its behavior, and when it gets into matters such as foreign policy and war, the historical lesson is that bad things get worse. The blindness, the ignorance, the stupidity, the folly, the arrogance, the narrowness, the rigidity, the inflexibility that led to the Vietnam mess did not come into the world in 1950. These qualities were present in superabundance during the Second World War and certainly in every previous war in which men have engaged.

The appalling thought is that there is no real way to guarantee that it won't happen all over again.

What did we learn from the Pentagon Papers that we did not already know? I do not mean, of course, that there are not *facts* the papers revealed to us which were previously known only to a very few Americans. I mean that the *lessons* of the Vietnam War were all known before and they did not prevent us from getting into it. If we had not learned them by 1960, what reason is there to think that we have learned them by 1970? How can we prevent the same things from happening all over again?

It might be said that the government should have learned not to lie to the people, but there is little reason to think that if all the secret decisions were revealed when they were made there would have been much difference in the public attitude toward the war. Even if Lyndon Johnson had announced before November of 1964 that the war in Vietnam would probably have to be expanded, he would still have beaten Barry Goldwater. Public disillusionment with the war was based on the fact that it went on too long and involved too heavy a price for something that did not seem worth it. It is extremely doubtful that any public in the world would be moved by arguments more sophisticated than that. It is not good to lie to the people. Dishonesty, be it that of Franklin Roosevelt in the 1940s or of more recent administrations in the 1960s, destroys the credibility of a government. The American people believed they were not being told the truth about the war long before Daniel Ellsberg's arrival on the scene. If everything in the Pentagon Papers had been released to the public a month after it had been written, it is extremely unlikely that the slow but implacable pace of public disenchantment with the war would have been much accelerated.

A second lesson might be that the American government should never get into long-term limited wars in faraway places where the casualty rates will be high and the national interest is not obvious. Such a rule is certainly a good one. Harry Truman would undoubtedly endorse it. But scarcely a decade after we ought to have learned this definitively in Korea we seem to have had to learn it all over again. Dean Rusk, in a television interview, lamented the fact that the war did not have the kind of public support necessary to see it through to a successful conclusion; but what in the world made Mr. Rusk think that such a war could sustain public support for very long? We have had to learn the lesson of Korea all over again. Maybe twice in a quarter century is enough to make the lesson stick, but it seems that man's capacity to learn from past mistakes is tragically limited.

Or, it may be urged, more attention should be paid to questions of morality in determining public policy issues; but, as Daniel Patrick Moynihan has observed, defending democracy in Southeast Asia is an exquisitely moral stance. It may not be mine or yours, but it is a moral stance. Few people are explicitly immoral. Harry Truman justified the bomb on Hiroshima in terms of the lives it would save, both American and Japanese, compared to the lives lost if an invasion of the islands of Japan had been necessary. We may not like such a moral justification, but the problem about falling back on moral arguments is that one man's morality is another man's madness. Those who directed the war in Southeast Asia, it will be said, had little concern for human life, but they would surely reply that they had immense concern for human life; they were convinced it was necessary for the United States to take the stand it did so that many millions of human lives would not be blotted out when all the dominoes fell over. One fights a limited war, the argument goes, in order to avoid a total war. I am not saying that I accept this argument or that I agree with its morality. I am saying that while concern for morality and respect for human life are admirable, they do not automatically dictate policy decisions. It is not hard to find moral rationalizations for almost any policy decision, and, beyond that, men of sincerity, integrity, and good will can disagree endlessly on what moral policy is. We have had few more moral secretaries of state than John Foster Dulles, and as the Pentagon Papers make clear, he was of decisive importance in the beginnings of America's post-Geneva involvement in Vietnam.

It is frequently asserted that the United Sates did not have a clearly thought-out foreign policy; but the Pentagon Papers make it clear that we did have a policy. It was called "containment" when George Kennan first enunciated it back in the forties and then it became known as "collective security," and then, more recently, the "domino" theory. It was a vigorous, consistent, well-thought-out policy, and in many respects it was a successful one. Western Europe was preserved, the expansion of the Soviet empire was prevented, and the slow breakup of Communist unity may very well have been facilitated by the check to Russian ambitions. I do not at this point wish to get into a detailed argument about the successes and failures of post-World War II foreign policy, particularly in Europe. I simply want to assert that the policy, was viewed as successful by most sections of the American public and even by most members of the liberal intellectual establishment. One wonders, for example, why the New York *Times* does not reprint some of its own editorials of the late fifties and the early sixties. Would we find in them any more serious questioning of the "collective security" approach than we find in the Pentagon Papers? This is not to criticize the *Times,* but merely to suggest that we did indeed have a policy, a policy that was endorsed by almost everyone. In retrospect, we stuck to the policy too long and applied it in times and circumstances where it was not only not pertinent but devilishly dangerous. But that, of course, is the problem with policies. One never knows when to abandon them, and the record of the human race generally forces us to the conclusion that policies are almost always abandoned when it is too late.

It might be suggested that what we need is more intelligent men in government. Surely no one can read the Pentagon Papers with the perspective that hindsight gives and not conclude that there was a vast amount of stupidity in the American government during the 1950s and the 1960s, and yet the level of academic and administrative intelligence in the American government during the Kennedy and Johnson years was probably higher than it had ever been before in the nation's history. Was there ever a time when there were more Ph.D.s in the federal government or more Harvard men or more men who could claim to be intellectuals? The intellectual community is now eager to repudiate the war quite possibly because it is all too aware that some of its most distinguished members must bear a heavy burden of responsibility for having gotten us into it. If there is any lesson to be learned at all about intellectuals in government from the Pentagon Papers, it is that it is probably a good thing to keep them out.

I don't really believe that, but I wonder whether that astute domestic politician Lyndon Johnson would have proceeded down the path to political disaster if he had not felt intellectually inferior to the brilliant Ph.D.s from Harvard who were advising him on foreign policy. Looking back, what might have been appropriate would have been more political shrewdness and less intellectual brilliance.

But perhaps we will solve the problem if we build into the government a system which guarantees that there are men who will say no. However, the Pentagon Papers make clear that there were "no" men all along the way. General Taylor, for example, did not like the "search and destroy" strategy. George Ball opposed involvement in the war.

Roger Hillsman opposed its escalation. Even McNaughton and McNamara came eventually to disagree, but they had sold the President on a policy and the policy was now being carried out by Westmoreland and the President. It was not for lack of hearing the opposite side of the question that the Vietnam tragedy came into being. At one point, it would seem, the President may have stopped listening to everyone but the military, but apparently that period did not last very long. What was lacking, perhaps, was a man of the influence in Johnson's administration that Robert Kennedy had in the prior one. Such a man of political shrewdness and historical perspective combined with a very high position in the decision-making structure is probably an accident, however, and that is a very thin reed on which to build our hopes for the avoidance of more tragedy.

It is now clear to almost everyone that we should not have become involved in the Vietnam War. One must simply say that such clarity was enjoyed by very few people seven years ago. We will not make the Vietnam mistake again. Indeed, we will probably not make a mistake even similar to it again, but given the folly of man, the complexity of the human condition, and the ever more sophisticated power of self-destruction available to us, do we have any reason to believe that we will not make other mistakes equally as bad if not worse? It is my melancholy conclusion that there is little reason to be hopeful about our capacity to avoid other equally serious tragedies in the future.

There are many confident people, however. One hears no more self-doubt from the critics of the men responsible for the documents in the Pentagon Papers than one can find in the documents themselves. There seems to be an abundance of men who are very sure of themselves, absolutely confident that they know what is to be done, and absolutely certain that their wisdom and their morality is superior to the wisdom and the morality of those who governed us in the sixties. I envy such men their confidence and their certainty. I do not, however, understand how they come by it, for in style if not in substance it is the same sort of certainty that marked the positions of "Bomber" Harris and W. W. Rostow. Sometimes I am prompted to think that the wisdom of a policy stands in inverse proportion to the confidence and the certainty of the men who advocate it.

How can those who so eagerly support new American policies in world affairs be so certain that disaster, suffering, and death will not follow from their policies, too? I am not saying we should not have new policies; on the contrary, it is clear that we should. I am simply saying that I am terribly uneasy in the presence of men who are convinced that they know the answers.

And I am troubled and confused by the unintended-consequence phenomenon which Liddell Hart saw so frequently in the Second World War. I wonder whether historians in the future will see a connection between the Vietnamese War and Mr. Nixon's bold steps toward a new policy toward China. Will the historians say that the Vietnamese tragedy was a necessary prelude to a long era of peace and good relations between the United States and China? Such a possibility suggests that human affairs are appallingly complicated and confused. A lot of straight lines may grow crooked in human affairs, but then occasionally it turns out that a crooked line may go straight.

Professor Brezenski has suggested that if the United States and the Soviet Union did not possess nuclear arsenals there would have almost certainly been a conventional war between the two countries sometime during the last quarter century. I do not know whether such an analysis is correct or not; in the nature of things, one cannot be sure, but it is a possibility, one that those who were so enthusiastic about unilateral disarmament might pause to consider.

One must take a stand, of course, for we cannot be so befuddled by the confusion and complexity of human events as to stand paralyzed before them, but we must be fully aware of the uncertainties, the complexities, the un-intended consequences, good and evil, and the possibilities of mistake that are inherent in the policies we advocate. We must also, it seems to me, be fully aware that we might be wrong and that those who disagree with us and criticize us may not only be in good faith but might also possess as much wisdom as we do—if not more.

Most human political policies fail. The only question is, how badly do they fail? What is desperately needed among both policy makers and critics is more self-doubt—not the self-doubt that paralyzes but the kind that makes us a little less than absolutely certain. I find the absence of doubt reprehensible in the men who wrote the Pentagon Papers. I also find it reprehensible in their critics. In the final analysis, the human race divides itself not into left or right, liberal or conservative, but into those who see the world as complicated, confused, uncertain, and am-biguous and those who see it as clear and simple. The latter are those who will destroy us all.

It is not enough to say merely that things are compli-cated. If we believe in a loving and gracious Reality, then there must be something that that belief contributes to our actions in moral situations, no matter how complex they might be.

CHAPTER 12

THE STYLE OF A BELIEVER

The follower of Yahweh living in the contemporary world must make his decisions in a context of great complexity and with the awareness that no matter how hard he tries, there is a good chance that he will make many mistakes. He also must come to understand that if the arguments presented in the last two chapters are correct, his religion does not provide him with a set of ready-made answers to all human problems. Rather, it gives him a world view, which shapes and colors the style of his behavior without necessarily prescribing the content of that behavior in a given situation.

The Yahwist may not do something that his pagan friends would do, and the reason may have little to do with a different moral code. A young person committed to the Sinai symbol is not likely to join his teen-age friends in stealing jeans from a clothing store, not because he knows the theft is wrong and they think it is right. Both they and he know it is wrong. A businessman at a convention may stay away from a house of prostitution to which his colleagues are going, not because he has a special revelation telling him that adultery is wrong. His colleagues know that infidelity is as wrong as he knows it is. The young person and the businessman act morally because their religious convictions provide them with more powerful motivations for moral action.

In other words, if you really believe that you are in a covenant with Yahweh, there are some sorts of things you simply don't do, because they are inappropriate for a member of the covenant community. While there is much moral complexity in the world, there are also many situations in which the difference between right and wrong is perfectly clear. Theft, murder, lying, adultery are wrong, and while it may not always be obvious what those things are, there are many times when it is obvious. The Yahwist avoids these sins not because he needs his religion to know that they are sinful or even because he expects Yahweh to come down from Sinai in fire and thunder to destroy him for his sins. Rather he is conscious of just the sort of person the covenant makes him. He understands that there are some kinds of behavior that clearly and explicitly violate the terms of the covenant.

What Yahweh said in the specifically moral stipulations of the covenant was, in effect, "You didn't need me to tell you that theft, murder, and adultery were wrong. You knew without me that you shouldn't do those things. I am saying now that if you are one of my people, you will follow your own sound moral instincts and cease those sorts of activities, for they are beneath the dignity of those who have entered into covenant with me."

But we are dealing with prohibitions. It is frequently quite clear what a follower of Yahweh will not do. When faced with certain options he will have no doubt that there are some he ought not to choose. It is much more difficult, however, for him to discover what positively he should be doing. As I remarked in the previous chapter, moral principles may be useful for deciding what kind of foreign policy not to engage in, but they are much less useful in indicating what sort of positive foreign policy one should develop. Similarly, on the level of the individual person, the thirteenth verse of Chapter 20 of Exodus describes outer limits beyond which no Yahwist will go. However, what positive actions he will take within those limits is mostly up to him. Some of his positive decisions will be the same as those of his pagan friends and neighbors and yet different from some fellow Yahwists of sincerity, intelligence, and good will.

It would be quite possible, for example, that for reasons exactly the same as those arrived at by non-believers, a young Yahwist would refuse to serve in the war in Vietnam. At the same time, it would be possible for an equally committed, equally sincere believer to decide that, however many evils may have been associated with the war, it is his duty to serve there. We ought not to be surprised that those who are of the household of faith may differ on specific applications of moral issues. Indeed, we had better become accustomed to such differences, because they are likely to increase rather than decrease in our increasingly complex moral situations.

I am not suggesting that both decisions are of equal moral value or that both young men have with equal accuracy evaluated the situation about which they are deciding. In the objective order, one man has made a correct judgment about the war and another man an incorrect one. My own inclinations are to think that the first young man was accurate in his evaluation, but it is the nature of the complexity and ambiguity of decisions which must be made on such issues that it is very difficult for anyone to be certain at the present time which decision was correct. In order to make my point as vigorously as possible, let me say that I can envisage a situation in which the man who refuses to serve in the war is less moral than the one who serves eagerly and enthusiastically. If he who refuses to serve is arrogant and righteous about his own goodness, if he has contempt for those who decide differently, if he makes sweeping judgments about whole classes of people from the heights of his own superior moral rectitude, if he converts his own agonized and difficult moral choice into a "formula religion" which guarantees him "peace of soul," if he thinks that he is now excused from any further efforts at religious and moral growth and that he is dispensed from further generosity, openness, and trust with his fellow human beings, then for all the correctness of his moral judgment, he is not part of Yahweh's covenant. He has responded to a gracious God not with graciousness in his own personal life but with narrowness, rigidity, and pride.[1]

On the other hand, he who decides that it is his duty to serve in Vietnam may do so with the full consciousness that his decision could be wrong, with great humility and openness, with the willingness to change his mind and to learn and grow, and with a powerful commitment to respect and generosity in dealing with everyone, even those who are his enemies. We may have under such circumstances an incorrect reading of the context of a moral situation yet a style of behavior which is appropriate for a religiously committed person.[2]

To put the matter even more bluntly, the one who serves in Vietnam may return humble and uncertain. He may say, "I am no longer sure about the rectitude of my decision. I did the best I could under the circumstances. I may have been right, but I may also have been

[1] Let it be clear that I am not suggesting that such attitudes are characteristic of those who have decided not to serve in Vietnam. I am merely asserting that in such cases where these attitudes may be found, we may indeed have moral excellence but we do not have a follower of Yahweh.

[2] Of course it is possible for someone who decides to serve in the war to give way to self-pity, to be cruel and exploitive in his relationships with the people of the country, and to deteriorate morally, religiously, and humanly while in the combat area. My point is that neither objective decision necessarily guarantees religious or human growth.

mistaken. I will have to live with the uncertainty." The man who refused to serve may go through the rest of his life with the absolutely unshaken conviction that there is no doubt about his rectitude and the immorality of those who decided differently. I would have no hesitation in saying that the former young man is the more religiously admirable of the two.

I have deliberately chosen an example where at the present time the sympathy of most readers will be with the one who refuses to serve in the war to illustrate as powerfully as I can my point that in areas of great moral ambiguity and complexity what distinguishes the religious is not so much the substance of a decision as its style. It is more religiously admirable to make a mistake with a style of graciousness, openness, and love than to be right with a style of arrogance, rigidity, and contempt. Obviously, of course, the most desirable result of all is a decision which is both more morally appropriate than the other and also carried out with a style of graciousness and love.

But it is easier to spot the covenant moral style—if we may call it that—in action than to describe it theoretically. How ought one to behave if one views the world from within the context of the Sinai myth? All that can be done in this book is to present a sketchy outline of some of the characteristics of the covenant style.

1. *The person who is committed to the covenant is "secure" in his moral behavior.* He is not at all confident that he is immune from making mistakes. On the contrary, he is probably more willing than others to admit that he may be making mistakes, but his sense of worth and dignity as a human person is not rooted in his perfection. He can more readily come to terms with his fallibility because he realizes that his worth and value are not negated by it. Yahweh has made covenant with obviously fallible people; he apparently does not consider that to

be an obstacle to *hesed*. If Yahweh can live with our weakness and proneness to mistakes, then, presumably, we can live with them too.

We do not enjoy making mistakes; we are not complacent about the incorrect moral decisions we make, but neither are we obsessed by them. Furthermore, since we are capable of admitting our errors of moral judgment—to say nothing, of course, of our sinfulness—we are also capable of learning from our mistakes and of evaluating decisions that were made with sincerity but with improper readings of all the circumstances. The Yahwist is less concerned about proving his own blamelessness than he is about understanding what happened, learning from it, and growing in personal wisdom so that a similar mistake will not be committed. He is sorry for his mistakes and sorry for the sinfulness, such as it may have been, which resulted from them. But he is not paralyzed by guilt. If the gracious God who loves him is willing to forgive—and there is nothing clearer in both the old and the new covenants than that God is only too willing to forgive— then the follower of Yahweh is willing to accept forgiveness and begin his life again, sadder but wiser. Because he is secure in his covenant with Yahweh, he does not fall apart under the strain of mistakes and sinfulness.

Let us take an extreme example to make the point. A man and woman, each is a reasonably happy relationship with their respective spouses, are brought together in the context of their work. They enjoy each other's company and become good friends. The attraction grows more powerful and they find that, while they continue to give their marriages prime importance, this new relationship is also deeply meaningful to them emotionally. One evening a crisis in their company forces them to work overtime, and when they finally leave the office they pause for one and then several drinks. Almost before they know what is happening they are in a hotel room together committing what must certainly be called adultery, though at the moment of action they are suffused with enormous pleasure and joy. The next day the two are utterly overwhelmed with shame. Neither has ever been unfaithful before. Both are convinced that they have desecrated what were fundamentally happy marriages. They are paralyzed by guilt over what they have done and they wonder how they can possibly expiate the ugliness of their sin.

I would argue that it is precisely at this point that religious issues become paramount. Shame is an appropriate emotion; what they have done is shameful. But guilt and emotional paralysis are not appropriate at all and may be counterproductive, because guilt is likely to weaken a marriage now suddenly perceived as threatened and to force the two people closer to one another in a continuation of the adulterous relationship, a continuation which might not occur if they were able to move beyond guilt and self-reproach to understanding and self-forgiveness.

If these two people are firmly convinced of Yahweh's love for them, they should be capable of leaving the exact measurement of their blame to God. It may very well be, to use the old pre-Vatican category, that what they did was no more than venially sinful. They were caught in a concatenation of circumstances and events which, temporarily at least, deprived them of their full freedom and were swept along by impulses and passions of which they were only dimly aware and over which they had very little control. On the other hand, it may be that for a long time the two of them had been kidding themselves and each other about the nature of their relationship; even a little bit of objectivity would have warned them that they were skidding toward unfaithfulness. But the point is that in the shame of the morning after they are in no position to decide. They may never be in a position to decide. What they did was certainly not done, to use the old terms, "with full and free deliberation," but neither were they absolute slaves to forces beyond their control. They have no rational choice, then, but to live with the realization that their culpability is indeterminate. They are not the greatest sinners that ever lived. On the contrary, they may be only relatively minor sinners, but neither are they completely free from sinfulness.

Since they can do no more about determining their precise guilt, the appropriate question to ask is, what did the incident reveal about themselves, their personalities, and their relationships with their spouses and with each other? They must also ask themselves and each other what sort of mistakes they might panic into because of the neurotic guilt that becomes terribly intermingled with the authentic shame that they both feel. In other words, it is much more constructive to ask, What mistakes did we make? Why did we make them? What can we learn from them? than it is to ask, How guilty are we? Expiation consists more of intelligent analysis and growth in understanding than in self-torment. Obviously, mistakes were made that brought them to the hotel room and obviously, there was sinfulness involved; but the mistakes do not have to be repeated, nor does their shame have to lead to other mistakes. Their sin, paradoxically enough, provides them with the opportunity for religious and personal growth, for becoming better human beings, better marriage partners, and, quite possibly, even better friends. They expiate their sin not by yielding to overpowering guilt, not by imposing the burden of knowledge on their spouses, but by honestly and realistically facing themselves, asking what mistakes were made, and determining how the mistakes arose.

Obviously, it is not easy to respond to such a difficult, traumatic, and complicated moral crisis with confidence and the self-possession that I described in the past paragraphs. One has to be willing to admit that one is a sinner and that one is still lovable. One has objectively violated a precise stipulation of the covenant, but if one really believes in the covenant, one knows that he is not excluded from the covenant because of this violation, that on the contrary it is incredibly easy to remain part of the covenant despite one's sinfulness. If Yahweh is ready to remit sinfulness, then the sinner must also be ready to remit it. This does not mean that he did not sin; it does mean that his sin neither destroys him nor deprives him of the amazing lovability that Yahweh sees in him. The Yahwist's faith symbol enables him to accept himself as a sinner, transcend the sinfulness, and, in an echo of the Easter liturgy *O felix culpa*, profit from his sin.

The old moral theology would have insisted that the two sinners "separate" immediately. One or the other would have to seek employment elsewhere. But such a quick answer, while in some circumstances appropriate, may in other circumstances not be. It may turn out that the two people are sufficiently able to evaluate and to understand what happened so that they know that they can continue the relationship without a repetition of the incident and without endangering their other and more important commitments. All they can do in the circumstances is to try with as much sincerity and intelligence as they can to make a tentative decision. They must face the fact that their relationship has been changed; their friendship has manifested itself once in a physical union that they could not help but enjoy. This intimacy, even though they are ashamed of it, is a fact of their relationship that they will be unable to change and which will have an influence of its own on the continuation of the relationship. They will have to integrate into their friendship the factuality, the pleasurability, and the shamefulness of the hotel room experience. To be able to do this will require not only a great deal of personal emotional maturity but also a great deal of faith. The covenant symbol should facilitate such an integration, but it will certainly not make it easy.

Can they be sure that the incident will not be repeated? Obviously they cannot; nobody can be sure of anything. Even if it should be repeated, the repetition would not make them unable to receive Yahweh's saving and forgiving love. It would mean sin, shame, and the need for a far more rigorous evaluation of the chain of events that led to the repetition. It would certainly indicate that now there is at least a reasonable presumption that the relationship is too risky to continue. Even a repetition of the sin—to whatever extent it was a sin—could still be turned into an opportunity for religious and personal growth if the two people had deep enough faith in God's love for them.

I deliberately describe in detail this imaginary (though hardly infrequent) event to emphasize that the covenant symbol does provide powerful personal resources for responding to the experience of one's own sinfulness and one's own inadequacies in evaluating the circumstances of moral decision making. The Yahwist can live with his mistakes; he can even learn from them.

2. *The man who is committed to the covenant symbol strives to respect the personhood of all of those in the moral context in which he acts.* He may offend some, he may have to defend himself against others, but he does so without either denying their humanity or turning them into objects which he can use for his own pleasure or as pretexts for his own selfishness. Furthermore, he is aware that the tendency to objectify and to blame others is present in all of us and affects our moral behavior and decision making. It is not so much a question of eliminating exploitation and scapegoating from our personalities as recognizing them, allowing for them, and limiting their influence.

Presumably, the couple described above will have to face the fact that to some extent they were exploiting one another. They were not merely enjoying free and open friendship, they were seeking something from the relationship that they were not finding in their marriages. Perhaps this "something" was lacking in their marriages precisely because they were not "free and open" enough in that relationship. They may have been "using" one another because they had been "using" their respective spouses. On the "morning after," they may be powerfully tempted to continue the exploitation either by heartlessly dropping the other now that one had achieved the aim of exploitation or, more probably, continuing the relationship without facing its exploitive component and at the same time actively and more directly pursuing more exploitation.

There may be at the same time a strong tendency for them to project their own guilt onto others. The transference of blame from oneself to someone else is pervasive in human relationships, particularly in intense and intimate ones. Blaming the other is a form of exploitation and objectification—which in its turn justifies more exploitation and objectification. It is dishonest, cheap, and snide, but anyone who thinks he is immune from it is only kidding himself.

The Sinai covenant makes it clear that Yahweh is only too ready to forgive sin, but it also makes it clear that, passionate God that he is, he will not tolerate hypocrisy. Exploitation and scapegoating are forms of hypocrisy. Rarely do we exploit others explicitly (though sometimes the rationalizations and justifications for exploitation are so transparent that we know the exploiter isn't even fooling himself), but all of us are tempted to "use" our parents, our children, our friends, our lovers, our spouses, our colleagues, our superiors, and our subordinates. It is terribly difficult to deal with another subject—a person with hopes, aspirations, fears, and anxieties like our own. We turn others into objects because they are so much less frightening when we can depersonalize them. Prostitution is a classic example of objectification. Physical pleasure can be enjoyed without the messiness of trying to relate to another subject. Prostitution is only a caricature of the objectification and exploitation that pervades our lives. Yahweh may love us all as persons, but we find it terribly difficult to cope with the responsibility of being part of a covenant community in which we must covenant with others as Yahweh has convenanted with us. The strain of dealing with our role opposites as subjects—while at the same time not giving ourselves over to maudlin bathos —is extremely wearing. We can probably only tolerate the strain if others support us both by treating us like subjects and challenging and encouraging us to deal with them and with everyone as subjects. It is for this purpose that we have a covenant community, and in the new covenant it is for this purpose that we have a Church. The Church is nothing else but a group of human beings trying to support one another in the difficult challenge of responding to Yahweh's gracious love by being graciously loving to everyone with whom Yahweh has peopled our environment.[3]

3. *He who has committed himself to the covenant symbolism is able to be humble in his moral behavior.* He is quite conscious that he does not have all the answers. He is aware of his own mistakes and is able to accept them and try to learn from them. He acknowledges that he has no necessary monopoly either on knowledge or on moral insight and that others may be both more accurate in their evaluation of situations and more courageous in their personal decisions—even though he does not confuse accepting extreme positions with moral wisdom.

[3] For a discussion of this concept of the Church as a community supporting us in our efforts to deal with others as subjects rather than objects, as persons rather than things, see my book, *What a Modern Catholic Believes About the Church,* Chicago: Thomas More Press, 1972.

He who believes in the Sinai myth has strong and unassailable notions about the graciousness of God's love, but because the strength of his religious commitments is so powerful, he is able to listen to and learn from others. His humility is obviously related to the personal security we discussed previously. He finds that his value and his worth does not depend on the invariable correctness of his moral judgments but on Yahweh's love. Furthermore, his humility is also grounded in his respect for others as persons. Since the others are subjects, not objects, they are capable of knowledge and insight and wisdom, and they must be listened to instead of being dismissed out of hand. The follower of Yahweh has enough personal and religious strength from his own commitment that he is able to listen to others.

Unlike certain varieties of the species *Liberalis academicus,* the member of the covenant community feels under no constraint to accept the moral perspectives and decisions of others and make them his own—especially when the moralities of the others are stated with deep and powerful passion. The Yahwist, unlike the liberal faddist, has convictions of his own, but precisely because he is secure he is able to listen to others, perhaps to learn from them, and certainly understand them in the context of their own backgrounds and ultimate symbol systems. Similarly, he has no need to try to impose his morality or his symbols upon others. He will explain them with all the vigor at his command, and he will argue about his own moral convictions and decisions with as much integrity and persuasiveness as he possesses, but neither his faith nor his morality depend on the acceptance of others and therefore he has no need to constrain others to agree with him. He knows where the ground is on which he stands and is confident of the value of that ground even if there are others who refuse to stand on it. He does not arrive either at his religious symbols or at his moral decisions by counting noses. If others wish to move their noses and their brains to another religious and moral position, the Yahwist does not feel the need, much less the compulsion, to abandon his position. His strength comes not from the consent of others nor from his ability to impose his will on others nor from the ease with which he can turn others off when they disagree with him; it comes from the covenant that he knows Yahweh has entered with him.

4. *The man who believes in the covenant symbol has no need to become a Grand Inquisitor. He does not succumb to the temptation to "do good."* He does not go around attempting to protect others from their ignorance or sinfulness. He does not view his mission in life as saving others from the misuse of their freedom. Yahweh gave freedom to all men and to each man; it is between Yahweh and the other person what sort of relationship the two of them develop. A man committed to the Sinai myth knows damn well that he can't force Yahweh into anything. He also understands that Yahweh is not going to accept any attempt to force another of his servants into anything. The covenant is a free commitment on both sides, and those who attempt to force others into it do so at the risk of discovering that they are not really part of the covenant themselves. The missionaries who converted the Chinese with the promise of rice, the kings who brought their whole people into the Church, the pastors who "train" everyone in the grammar school to go to confession on the Thursday before First Friday, the parents who force their children to attend Sunday Mass all have one thing in common: unlike Yahweh, they are not prepared to permit people to be free. One must conclude that the Sinai myth did not have a very powerful hold on their religious and moral lives.

5. *The convinced Yahwist claims freedom not only for himself and his kind but for all men.* The sabbath commandment proclaims rest not only for the children of

Israel but for their slaves and for the strangers who are living in their camp. Some commentators think that the word used in the commandment "Thou shalt not steal" means "Thou shalt not steal thy neighbor's freedom," that is to say, "Thou shalt not turn your neighbor into a slave." Furthermore, the denunciation of false witnesses seems to be aimed at dishonesty in legal and quasi-legal proceedings. Thirteen centuries after Sinai, Jesus would rail against injustice, oppression, and hypocrisy; and the Israelite and Christian religious traditions at their best are in constant protest against oppression and injustice. Unfortunately, some members of both traditions, particularly (sad to say) the Christian tradition, have permitted themselves to become so identified with the status quo in its various times and places that they have become not merely part of oppressive social structures but vigorous defenders of such oppression.

One need not go as far as the so-called "political theologians," who argue that the Church must criticize everything and that the essential role of the Church is social criticism. One cannot escape the conclusion, however, that those who believe that Yahweh has entered into covenant with his people must be horrified at the thought that the people of Yahweh—now understood to be the whole human race—are anywhere in the world victims of tyranny, injustice, and oppression. Outrage at oppression is not the same thing as advocacy of simplistic solutions to social problems; and passion to expand human freedom is not the same thing as self-righteous denunciation of those who, despite serious efforts, have not been able to eliminate injustice. The fight against tyranny and oppression is a long one, and as we have suggested, a complicated one. It is not likely to become completely successful in our day or perhaps ever until the Day of Yahweh comes. But if those who believe in the Sinai myth realize that social reform requires competence, patience, skill, persistence, and perseverance, they also must understand that given the covenant symbol which has enveloped them they have no choice but to be angry and appalled at the things man is still doing to his fellow men. If it is necessary—and I am convinced that it is—to insist that much that passes as Christian social criticism is naïve and romantic, it is also necessary to insist that sophisticated social criticism and long-range commitment to social reform are not adequate for the follower of Yahweh unless they are combined with passion and anger at the fact that men still stand in the way of Yahweh's graciousness.

It is difficult, of course, to combine passion with sophistication; the young are more likely to be passionate, the old more likely to be sophisticated, and those of us who stand in between are, alas, unlikely to possess enough of either quality. Yet because it is difficult to combine anger and an awareness of complexity, it does not follow that those who are committed to the Sinai covenant are excused from their obligation to try to combine both qualities. Those whose lives have been grasped by the covenant symbol are men and women who are permanently committed both to enthusiasm and excellence, the former because they understand the secret of Yahweh's love, and the latter because nothing less is an appropriate response to his loving graciousness.

6. *The Yahwist takes risks.* Because he is confident of the fundamental graciousness of the universe, he knows that it is not necessary to play everything safe, and while he is not an incorrigible gambler who must risk everything, he still understands that human, personal, and religious growth occurs only when one is willing to take intelligently reasoned chances. Since he knows that in the long run nothing can separate him from Yahweh's love, he knows that even when he seems to lose, he really doesn't.

One of the besetting problems of upper-middle-class

American youth—particularly those whose parents spent
their formative years in the Great Depression—is their inability to risk themselves. Fear of making decisions about
career, marriage, and children and their reluctance to
expose their total selfhood in complete and enthusiastic
dedication to what they are doing are widespread among
American young people. They constitute the most serious
problem that the counselors and therapists who deal with
college and graduate school students must face. Many
young people find it much easier to be content with un-
imaginative mediocrity, within which one can argue that
one has never really failed, than to take the big risks,
which, indeed, give one the opportunity for success but
also force upon one the risks of failure. I have known
doctors, lawyers, poets, journalists, and sociologists who
are content with "just getting by," because anything more
than that is entirely too risky. I have also known young
people who make great progress in understanding and
insight in therapy, but resolutely refuse to act on their
understanding and insight because if they give up their
neurotic defenses they will have to take the risk of strain-
ing toward excellence, and in that risk is the possibility
of failure.

Such young people obviously did not acquire much self-
confidence in their families, and neither did they acquire
much faith in Yahweh. It is intolerable that anyone who
has put on the Sinai covenant should be content with
mediocrity. If Yahweh is gracious, if the universe is good,
then it is necessary that man live his life to the fullest.
A narrow, timid, small, unsatisfying existence is anathema.

There was once in moral theology a theory called
tutiorism. According to this theory, it was required that a
person always follow the "safer" moral course. Most theoretical moralists reject tutiorism as a practical basis
for moral actions, but an implicit version of it was an important part of our educations. "No one will ever go to

hell," we were told, "for doing the safe thing." Quite apart from the question of going to hell, the dictum was wrong because erring on the side of safety is no guarantee that we will adequately respond to that passionate, head-long God of ours.

There is one example of tutiorism, in practice if not in theory, that I mention, if somewhat hesitantly. There is in the modern world an increasing awareness of the variability of human friendship. Intense friendships are possible between people who are not married to one another without other fundamental commitments they may have being violated. These friendships are widespread, but they are, I think, an especially severe dilemma among celibate religious, who are wondering whether close friendships with obvious and at times powerfully sexual overtones are compatible with their celibate commitment.

I hesitate to comment on this question because it is still an obscure and difficult one, and I do not feel qualified to discuss it with any confidence. I am con-vinced that my friend Eugene Kennedy is correct when he says that these relationships are only for the mature and the self-possessed and are not to be sought as an end in themselves. I am also convinced that is is extremely easy to engage in self-deception in this area. Finally, I think such friendships are only possible without serious danger when the people who engage in them have no question or doubt about the permanency of their funda-mental commitment.

But with all these qualifications it still seems to me that it is necessary to make the point that although these relationships may have a certain amount of risk in them, it does not follow that they are evil and should be aban-doned. Because I have alluded in passing to such friend-ships in some of my other writings, I receive some mail from people in such relationships who are plainly troubled.

It is very difficult, indeed, impossible, to make any intelligent comments on a particular relationship when one
does not know the people involved. But insofar as one
can make a judgment from a letter, I often find myself
convinced that the relationships described to me were
not only quite harmless but also making an important
positive contribution to the personal and religious growth
of the people involved and to the exercise of their apostolic
vocations. I could understand their troubles, for their
feelings sometimes were quite strong and led to displays
of affection of which they were, I think, deeply ashamed.
Furthermore, almost in the nature of those relationships,
there were few if any friends they could turn to for
support in working out the problems involved.

However, occasionally it seemed that the people involved had every reason to be confident that they would
neither end up in bed with one another or leave the
ministry. What tormented them and prevented them from
enjoying the blessings of their friendships was the fear that
they were doing something risky or unsafe. They felt it
would be *safer* to terminate the relationship altogether.

Unquestionably, it would be safer, but as is evident in
this chapter, safety of itself is not an appropriate criterion
to determine human moral behavior. Whether the calculated risk in the relationship is worth sustaining because
of the obvious benefits of that relationship to the people
involved is a decision which must be made in each case
by the two people. No universal principle can save them
from the agony of working out a decision for themselves.
However, once they have made their decision, it seems
that it would be appropriate for them to put aside their
worries and to continue with their work and their affection for one another. What if something goes wrong? they
may ask. To which one is forced to reply that something
may go wrong in any human relationship or, indeed, in

any human endeavor; and if "things go wrong" despite reasoned, mature caution to prevent such an occurrence, then one must simply evaluate the situation again. Worrying about the possibility of things going wrong can easily be a self-fulfilling prophecy and in any case it violates the trust and confidence which should be characteristic of the moral behavior of those who are committed to the Sinai myth.

I suspect that there are some readers who will go over these paragraphs word for word, looking for a "solution" to a "problem" they are facing. But no matter how often they reread this section they will find no solution for their problems. I do not believe that these relationships should be defined as problems. They are challenges, and how people respond to the challenge is up to them, not to me. All I am saying is that in this set of circumstances, as in every other, neither general principles nor a practical version of tutiorism excuses us from the agonizing and ambiguous responsibility of forming our own consciences and making our own decisions.

7. *Those who embrace the covenant symbol realize that they are never excused from effort.* If you believe in a gracious God and a universe that is "out to do you good," you are simply never allowed to quit. There are some situations and some relationships that may well be beyond redemption. One should be most reluctant to abandon a marriage commitment, for example, but it is a sad and inescapable fact that some marriages simply cannot be salvaged. Some pastors will never learn how to be friends with their junior colleagues; some superiors will never be able to be secure in the presence of their subordinates. Some employers will never be able to deal honestly with their employees. Some delinquents are incorrigible. Some sick people will not be helped by either surgery or therapy. No matter how much time, energy, and work we

put in there are still many times in our lives when we lose. The intelligent man knows when he has lost and goes away to try again somewhere else.

Nevertheless, to abandon hope for reconciliation or its functional equivalent must be done only very reluctantly and certainly not because one has been beaten once or has lost once or has taken a chance once and been rejected. The committed Yahwist does not think he is excused from trying again. If the universe is gracious, if Yahweh loves us, then we are committed to improvement—to improving ourselves, to improving our relationships, to improving the world. We must be under no illusions that it will be easy; it will require work, energy, discipline, sacrifice. And those efforts cannot be ends in themselves; they are means to other and more noble ends; they are transfused and transformed by a commitment to goodness by way of a full acceptance of a universe that is gracious and loving. The Yahwist does not run away. Just as Yahweh did not quit when Israel whored with false gods, so his follower does not resign from the fray when the going gets tough.

8. *Perhaps the most obvious manifestations of the Yahwist's moral style are a refusal to hate and a commitment to joy.* Those who believe in Sinai can grow very angry, not merely at ideas or at principles but at people. They may even find that they have no choice but violence, though they are most reluctant to do so. No matter what happens, they simply cannot hate for very long. It may well be true that others have done them great evil, but the evil is transient and Yahweh's loving graciousness is permanent. If Yahweh does not hate us because of our evil, then we are surely in no position to hate others because of their evil. This is a hard saying. Hatred is one of the most beloved of human possessions and we are reluctant to give it up. Most of us, I suspect, keep lists of our enemies and wait eagerly for the appropriate day

when we can "settle" with them.[4] Perhaps the measure of our lack of faith in the Sinai covenant is the amount of hatred still lingering in our personalities—limiting, constricting, deadening. It is precisely because hatred persists—and its principal ally, fear—that we are unable to be joyful. For joy is the ultimate mark of the follower of Yahweh. We can go forth to do battle with the Amorites (these now lurking inside ourselves instead of out on the desert) with a song on our lips only if we are confident that we have been possessed by a dazzling, gracious God. If there is no joy in our hearts, if we are frightened, narrow, angry, anxious men and women, then we have not put on the Sinai symbol; we have not really committed ourselves to the covenant myth, and we don't really believe, at least not with nearly enough strength, that our God does in fact love us.

My list of the characteristics of Yahwist moral behavior is obviously only a very tentative beginning. But the list shows that the covenant myth, even though it is not explicitly concerned with ethical systems and even though it does not provide precise answers to the many specific moral problems we face, nonetheless has extraordinarily important implications for human moral behavior. The security, reverence for persons, humility, moral outrage, courage, durability, trustfulness, and joy of the committed Yahwist ought to make him someone who clearly stands out among his fellow men.

If not many committed Yahwists stand out among their fellow men now, I suppose the reason is that not very many of us are all that committed to the God who revealed himself on the fruitful mountain.

---

[4] I will admit that I have such a mental list. (Some people I know actually have the list written out.) Alas for my Gaelic ire, whenever I encounter such an enemy in person, it vanishes. How foolish of me to be angry at them in the first place.

CHAPTER 13

COVETOUSNESS

> You shall not covet your neighbor's house: you
> shall not covet your neighbor's wife, or his male or
> female slave, or his ox or his ass, or anything that is
> your neighbor's. (Exodus 20:14)

The last two commandments, in the Catholic numbering
(the last one in the usual Jewish and Protestant numbering), forbids covetousness. One is not supposed to covet
either one's neighbors or one's neighbors' goods. The Hebrew word *hmd*, which is used here, does not usually
mean "admire" or "wish to have" but rather "to lay plans
to take." If one's neighbor has a surplus of goods or a
beautiful wife, it is not sinful to admire his possessions,
nor is it necessarily sinful to wish that one had equally
desirable possessions. Yahweh's stipulation rather is that
we do not permit ourselves to be so attracted by a neighbor's wife or goods that we lay plans to snatch them from
him.

The Israelite religious mind had a horror of covetousness quite possibly because in any closely knit community
one man's success is another man's failure. In the book
of Micah, Chapter 2, verses 1–2, the prophet powerfully
elaborates on the prohibition of covetousness by putting
the following words in Yahweh's mouth:

Woe to those who plot evil,
who lie in bed planning mischief!
No sooner is it dawn than do it
—their hands have the strength for it.
Seizing the fields that they covet,
they take over houses as well,
owner and house they confiscate together,
taking both man and inheritance.

In the pre-conciliar catechism, the ninth and tenth commandments were taken to be addenda to the sixth and seventh. Coveting our neighbor's wife meant "having dirty thoughts." Coveting our neighbor's goods meant envying his possessions. There never was very much concern about the tenth commandment in the old Church. We agonized at great length over the actual theft and had little time to worry over plans to steal. However, the detailing of the variety of offenses that could be committed through "impure thoughts" was extensive. While it was conceded that sexual fantasies (though the words were never used) were only sinful if one "consented to them," the impact on most religion classes about "impure thoughts" was such that most Catholics seemed to think that sexual fantasies had to be confessed in the sacrament of penance. How human beings could live in a world peopled by bodies approximately half of which were of the opposite sex and escape sexual fantasies was never made clear. In the moral theology books and the catechism, the ideal solution appeared to be to withdraw into a monastery where the half of the world's bodies of the opposite sex would never appear. A happy solution, and not quite so drastic, for many Catholics was to admit in the confessional that they had "dirty thoughts" but to affirm that "I didn't take any pleasure in them." Most of us who were confessors were willing to accept descriptions of mitigating circumstances without bothering to wonder how sexual fantasies could fail to be pleasurable, much less if there was much point in engaging in them if they weren't.

For all the *foolishness* to be found in this exaggerated moral rigorism, there was an important point, although those that made it rarely understood its full implications. The final stipulation of Yahweh deals not only with external human behavior but one's internal dispositions. But it is not the sixth and ninth commandments only that are underwritten by Yahweh's last stipulation; it is the whole Decalogue. It is applied not only to man's outward activity but also to his interior orientation. One of the Talmudic commentaries observed, quite appropriately, "He who violates the last commandment, violates all of them." If all of man's heart and mind are not given over to the covenant, then his external behavior is meaningless. Covetousness is a symptom that a man has not really put his trust in Yahweh; he still puts his trust in himself. He covets that which is his neighbor's even to the extent of planning to take it from his neighbor because he is not confident that Yahweh will honor the terms of the covenant and therefore believes that he must provide for himself. He is restless and dissatisfied with what he has and wants what someone else has because he believes that he can find security in his possessions. The one who has truly given his heart over to the covenant knows that security can come only from Yahweh.

The final stipulation of the covenant says the same thing as Father Shea, whom I quoted in another context earlier in this book, that it is not nearly enough to profess external faith in Yahweh's goodness. Man must rather take to himself the covenant commitment and permit it to permeate and pervade his whole being, so that his trust in Yahweh is not merely a matter of external assent but becomes a profound personal commitment that transforms everything he does. Until a symbol is internalized in that fashion, it really has not become a meaningful religious symbol at all. The final stipulation of the Decalogue demands that we internalize the covenant relationship by forbidding covetousness. No one who believes that Yahweh is his God is permitted to put his security in himself. The Yahwist does not covet because he does not need his neighbor's wife or goods for his own well-being and happiness. Certain as he is of Yahweh's love, there is no reason for him to scheme to take things from his neighbor.

This theme will recur in the New Testament. Commentators on the story of "the rich young man" tell us that the point made by that story is that the young man's problem was not so much the refusal to give up his possessions as it was the refusal to give up the personal security that the possessions provided. Indeed, Jesus' warnings against the perils of riches were not so much against material abundance in itself as rather the illusion of security that material abundance can give to the rich man (and by the standards of the New Testament, all but a tiny minority of contemporary Americans would be considered rich). There was no necessary merit in poverty in the teaching of Jesus, but the poor man could not delude himself into thinking that he was the master of his own fate. To this extent he was free from one of the self-deceptions possible to the rich—and possible to virtually everyone in a society where food, clothing, shelter, and medical care are relatively accessible to most of the population.

What Jesus criticized in the rich was what various prophets criticized in Israel's disastrous foreign policy. The Israelite kings thought that they could be secure and confident in their power if they made appropriate military alliances. The prophets warned them that the strength of the Israelites came not from military alliances but from Yahweh. When treaties became a substitute for the covenant of Yahweh Israel was doomed.

Neither in the Sinai covenant nor in the teaching of Jesus was there any mandate for personal or national irresponsibility. One is not to cease work in the fields under the assumption that Yahweh will provide manna. The point, rather, is not to delude oneself into thinking that even the most abundant harvest guarantees one's life or happiness. If one puts one's heart in the treasure of the harvest and if one's heart belongs to the harvest and not to Yahweh, he is not part of Yahweh's covenant.

The Yahwist works hard in the fields (or its functional equivalent in the modern world), and he hopes that the fields bear fruit because eating is better than starving, but he is not obsessively concerned about the harvest, for he knows that even if it fails, he will not be separated from Yahweh's love. Worry about the harvest is foolish because it will have no impact on the harvest and, more serious, it calls into question the sincerity and power of Yahweh's love.

If covetousness is defined as the conviction that we must rely on our own efforts, not merely to eat and to stay alive but also to justify the worth, dignity, and value of ourselves as human beings, there can be no doubt that covetousness is indeed a besetting problem for mankind, particularly in the modern, industrial societies, where one's worth is measured by wealth and success. Contemporary man must devote his thought to what he shall eat and what he shall drink and what he shall put on, because if his food and drink and clothing are not up to the expectations of his status, he can be written off as a failure. We covet not merely because we are not sure of Yahweh's gracious love, we also covet because our value and reputations as human beings depend upon the effect of our covetous behavior.

Much of the accumulation of wealth, pageantry, and

pleasures which may be observed in the world around us is rooted in psychological and human insecurity. We surround ourselves with goods and services to reassure ourselves of our worth and to protect ourselves from attacks by those who hate us. The accumulation of money we can never spend, goods we will never use, and pleasures we never really enjoy are all means of self-defense. They do not eliminate the reckoning of death or even postpone it. They give us the illusion that we are in control of our lives, that Yahweh does not hold us in the palm of his hand.

Partly by choice but mostly by chance, I live on the margins of a number of large institutions, neither a part of nor fully accepted by the Church or the academy. I used to flatter myself into thinking that the combination of decisions that moved me out on the margins was proof that I was a man of faith and could take the kind of risks that are expected from a servant of Yahweh. I am now more inclined to believe that there is also a strain of the compulsive gambler in me, and that the disaster of the Great Depression was so powerful an influence on my youth that my propensity for risk taking is evidence of my seeking an abundance of security that the world is incapable of providing. Deep down in my personality somewhere I want the absolute guarantee that the Great Depression won't occur again.

This line of thought occurred to me one day when a colleague remarked, "Greeley, you're the kind of man who enjoys doing things that bring people to the margins of society, but you don't like having to live there." The insight of this observation struck me very forcefully. As I look back over my life, I can see how the decisions I made inevitably pushed me to the margins. While there are obvious strategic advantages in freedom and flexibility and the independence that comes from marginality, I must confess that I find it difficult to live with the realization that I don't really belong anywhere. It seems to me that most people on the margins are not so bothered as I am by being exluded from full acceptance in both the Church and the university. The issue is complicated, and like everyone else, I am a jumble of confusing and contradictory emotions and motivations. I am not suggesting that all my life decisions have been primarily motivated by emotional insecurity and lack of faith. There is a strong and vigorous part of me that really enjoys the ambiguous role I play. I certainly would not give it up without a fight, but I would be kidding myself if I thought my "life project" was totally free from neurosis and infidelity.

I have lapsed into autobiography again because I cannot presume to judge any other man's motivations. I suspect that my experience is common enough. Most of our "life projects" are a combination of strength and weakness, of health and neurosis, fidelity and infidelity. If we had it to do all over again, we might very well make exactly the same decisions, but they would be purified from fear, insecurity, and the hoarding of treasures to protect us from the fragility and vulnerability of human existence. Rather than wishing that we could do it all over again, however, what we ought to do is face the infidelity in our lives and begin to reduce it. If my faith in Yahweh were strong enough, if I had given myself over to the covenant symbol more completely, I would not especially mind a life on the margins, because I would understand that all human beings live on the margin that stretches between birth and death, yet no man with whom Yahweh has bothered to covenant could possibly be marginal. Whenever I covet something to belong to, a "place of my own," I should remember that I do belong to something—a covenant. There is also a place of my own— at the foot of Sinai.

The final stipulation of the Decalogue, then, means that

Yahweh wants more than just external professions of confidence and trust; he also wants a confident and trusting heart, one that is so fundamentally secure in the graciousness of Being that it need not waste its time with foolish, trivial worries about wealth and pleasure. The Yahwist does not have the time and energy for such shallow concerns. The covenant has liberated him. He does not covet because he does not *need* to covet. He is free to devote himself to other, better things.

CHAPTER 14

THE END—THE BEGINNING?

There are those who wish to reconstruct the past and those who wish to destroy it. On the one hand, many Christians yearn for the "good old days" when the Ten Commandments were "taken seriously." On the other hand, there are Christians who wish to strike down the Ten Commandments as irrelevant.

The thesis of this book is that both positions are misguided. One can make no decisions about the Ten Commandments until one understands what they are. To reject them as an irrelevant moral code or to attempt to reconstitute them as a relevant one is fatuous activity if it turns out that they were never intended to be a moral code at all. The nineteenth and twentieth chapters of Exodus are not the beginning of an elaborate legal system; they are rather a record of a theophany, a manifestation by and an experience of the deity. The myths and the symbols which record the Sinai experience do not have whatever value they still possess because of their capacity to direct specific moral responses to specific moral issues. We investigate the Sinai symbols to see whether there is in them wisdom about the nature of the Real; whether, as Schubert Ogden has phrased it, they re-present to us our basic assurance of the purpose and worth of human life. In his book *What a Modern Catholic*

Believes About Heaven and Hell, Father John Shea describes the Catholic attitude toward religious symbols out of the past:

> There is a strong conserving strain in the Catholic tradition. The Christian is an incurable saver. He drags his whole past with him into the future. He would move quicker if he scrapped many of the things he carried, but he cannot bear to lose an alternative perspective or a possible truth. An ancient religious practice or a dusty doctrine may capture and communicate an undying aspect of the human situation. At the present moment its meaning may be obscure but that does not mean its truth is dead. The Christian hoards wisdom; he is reluctant to part with anything.[1]

The question that must be asked is whether the dry, old, dusty Decalogue may possibly contain a truth about the human religious situation that is timeless. Many of us may decide that the passionately aroused Yahweh of Sinai really has nothing to say about the nature of human existence, but if a decision is made to reject Yahweh, let him be rejected for that reason. It is foolish to turn Yahweh off because we don't like his commandments. If we are to turn him off, let us do so because we do not believe that Reality is that gracious and that loving.

But what happened to the Decalogue? How did it get converted into a stuffy, rigid legal code, when in fact it was initially a theophany? Paul Ricoeur has suggested that there is an almost incurable human tendency to make religious symbols the object of faith rather than the means of faith. We believe not in the reality that is revealed by the symbols but in the symbols themselves. The symbols cease to be means of communication between man and

[1] John Shea, *What a Modern Catholic Believes About Heaven and Hell.* Chicago: Thomas More Press, 1972.

God and become idols. From Ricoeur's point of view, we are presently engaged in an exercise of iconoclasm; we are smashing the idols so that we may recapture the symbols. But it is not enough to dispose of the idols. One must also examine the symbols almost, as it were, from the beginning.

> The situation in which language today finds itself comprises this double possibility, this double solicitation and urgency: on the one hand, purify discourse of its excrescences, liquidate the idols, go from drunkenness to sobriety, realize our state of poverty once and for all; on the other hand, use the most "nihilistic," destructive, iconoclastic movement so as to *let speak* what once, what each time, was *said*, when meaning appeared anew, when meaning was at its fullest. Hermeneutics seems to me to be animated by this double motivation: willingness to suspect, willingness to listen; vow of rigor, vow of obedience. In our time we have not finished doing away with *idols* and we have barely begun to listen to *symbols*. It may be that this situation, in its apparent distress, is instructive: it may be that extreme iconoclasm belongs to the restoration of meaning.[2]

The most critical issue vis-à-vis the Sinai symbols is revealed when we ask what they say to us about the nature of God, and of man, and of human life. When we pose the question this way, the answer may very well be that Sinai is absurd, but no one who has faced the challenge of the Sinai symbols can assert that they are irrelevant.

For the Yahweh whom we encounter at Sinai is not merely a God to be explained and understood. He is also

[2] Paul Ricoeur, *Freud and Philosophy: An Essay on Interpretation.* Translated by Denis Savage. New Haven: Yale University Press, 1969, p. 27.

a God demanding a response. All religious symbols, of course, demand some sort of response, but there is nowhere in the whole repertoire of human religious symbols one more insistent on a response than the Yahweh symbol. Paul Tillich puts the matter with his accustomed clarity and vigor:

> Man is always put before a decision. He must decide for or against Yahweh, for or against the Christ, for or against the Kingdom of God. Biblical ethics is not a system of virtues and vices, of laws and counsels, of rewards and punishments. All this is not lacking, but it appears within a framework of concrete, personal decisions. Every decision is urgent; it has to be made now. When it has been made, it has far-reaching consequences. It is always an ultimate decision—a decision of infinite weight. It decides man's destiny. It decides the destiny of nations, the selected one as much as the others. Every generation in every nation has to decide for or against righteousness, for or against him who is the God of righteousness. And in every nation, including the selected one, the decision against righteousness means self-destruction.[3]

We have two tasks: to listen to what Sinai says about Yahweh and, having heard the Sinai myth, to decide how we are going to respond to it.

It is difficult to listen to a symbol and avoid the extremes of re-creating idols or destroying the symbol. Our temptation is to strike out and destroy, particularly when we are angry at the tyranny that idols have exercised over our lives. We are suspicious of the Catholic tendency to hoard wisdom, and in our ignorance and suspicion we feel inclined to say, "To hell with it all! Let us start over and let the dead symbols of the past bury their dead."

[3] Paul Tillich, *Biblical Religion and the Search for Ultimate Reality*. Chicago: The University of Chicago Press, Phoenix Books, 1964, p. 45.

But if it is difficult to pass beyond iconoclasm to understanding, it is even more difficult to pass from understanding to faith. We may conclude our listening to the Sinai symbols with the willingness to concede that Yahweh is a fairly impressive God, but such a confession is not faith, and when we have the choice of taking the great leap of faith or going back to smashing idols, pushing the idols around seems a much less demanding enterprise. I am in no position to force anyone to make an act of faith, but as a follower of Yahweh, however inadequate my discipleship may be, I insist that he deserves a hearing at least. It is a monstrous distortion of who and what he is to think that the self-revelation which took place on Sinai was nothing more than the proclamation of a legalistic code. You don't have to like my God —and I admit that there are times when he is a terribly difficult sort of deity—but you should at least dislike him for the right reasons.

This volume is a sequel to my book *The Jesus Myth*, and I think that for Christians the order is appropriate. We first encounter Jesus and then through him come to explore the Old Testament and encounter his father, Yahweh, on Sinai. Once we have explored the Sinai myth, we are then faced with the difficult question of whether the cross and resurrection symbols add anything to the Sinai covenant symbol. The idea of personal resurrection, of a relationship between God and the individual person in addition to his relationship with the people, the emphasis on the universality of Yahweh's revelation, and even the insistence on unselfish love all antedated the coming of Jesus. Late Old Testament Judaism had concluded to a belief in resurrection and a personal relationship between God and individuals. It had also become universalistic in its higher theory, if not in practice. So the uniqueness of the Jesus event cannot be found in any of these phenomena.

But the question of what the resurrection adds to Sinai is an absurd one. How can you add to a revelation that says that God is passionately in love with his people, that the universe is not only benign and gracious but madly in love? Jesus did not say anything fundamentally new. He rather renewed the old theophany of Sinai.

But of course, to a Christian the symbol of the Jesus who died and now lives again adds richness, intensity, and detail to the Sinai symbols. The parables of Jesus describe even more elaborately than Sinai did the madness of our loving God. The cross and the resurrection are much more specific promises of the ultimate impact of Yahweh's love for us than the Sinai covenant contained. It is not a new Yahweh that we encounter in Jesus but rather a more highly developed, more explicitly stated, and more richly symbolized Yahweh. Jesus may not add anything to the fundamental message of God's love for us—for to that nothing can be added—but Jesus does represent the length and the breadth, the height and the depth of God's love. The marvelous thing about the Great Secret is that it is one we all knew from the beginning. Every human being perceives it dimly. Israel learned it more clearly in the desert around Sinai, and Jesus came into the world to tell us all that the Secret was really true, that it was all right to be surprised because the great surprise was yet to come.

And like his father Yahweh, he stands expectantly and says to us, "What are you going to do about that?"